Monster Child

By Kristal M. Johnson

With Love

To my Dad. *Who showed me how to love and live and write, in that order.*

Hal Hostetler, 1933-2017

Contents

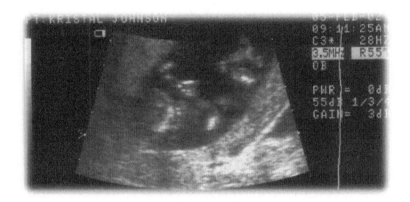

Konner, three months in utero, February 2002

Chapter 1

Monstrous Behavior

Konner, 2, and Brennig, 9 months, playing, 2004

"Mama!" cries Brennig, palms to his ears. "Why are we here?"

The screams behind me are making my eardrums wobble with pain: Konner's screams. I rest my arm on the back of my seat and half turn. "It's okay, baby," I say to

5

Brennig, who sits in the back of the SUV. "You just stay put."

He's two years old, younger than the creature screaming beside him, and his blue-gray eyes are teary under his winter hood.

Konner's head is practically spinning around. He's possessed, I swear, arching his back and kicking his boots, screaming like someone is torturing him.

I won't be able to do it from here.

With the car still running I push out the door, met by a bright cold slap of air. I'm a good mom. I am. I hope I am. And it's hard to believe what I'm going to do.

In the window I catch a glimpse of myself: my long smooth hair and a face that's trim but frazzled, upset. So different from the fun and driven person I used to be.

I slam the door and crunch over the crumbling gravel to open his door.

I peer inside with my arms crossed, shivering inside my knee-length coat, waiting for his screams to peter out. He knows I'm here. I know he knows. Even with eyes squeezed shut, he knows.

I can sense the low-lying hills around us and all the cars that are rumbling past on the road behind me, accusing me. That this isn't the way to handle things. But something has to be done. It does. I can't keep living life like this.

I reach for Konner's buckle.

"No!" He blocks my hand. And gives me a sharp suspicious look.

I feel the heat pumping off his face, his plump pink cheeks, and sweaty blond hair. "You need to get out of the car," I say. This little intervention worked for a friend, whose daughter kept screaming inside the car, so I'm praying it's going to work for us, too.

Konner turns his head to see where we are. "This isn't our house."

"I know it's not. But it's where you get out."

He shakes his head furiously and I lean in close to unbuckle his belt.

He swings at me.

"Konner!" I jump back, shocked.

He gives me a dark and furious look, then lets out a shriek.

"I'm tired of this. Do you hear me, Konner? I can't stop the mean things you do. But the fire department has other mamas who'll know what to do. They'll take much better care of you. It's time to get out."

He shakes his head.

"I'm sorry," I say. "But you need to get out." I reach for his straps.

He screeches and swings and punches my arm. Bam-bam, bam-bam!

Startled, I stagger away from him, my heart thumping against my ribs. My forearms throb where he punched me, hard, and I feel like dissolving into tears right there, in front of a child who's only three.

I hold my arms protectively. All I needed to do was to get Konner out of the car. To scare him into thinking I can't handle his tantrums and his moods (I can't), then explain he can only come home if he's going to stop acting this way.

And by *acting this way*, I mean *every* day.

But now, he's hit me. I'm fighting back a lava-like flow of tears.

I'm a failure, I think, with this awful kid. I can't even handle a single intervention and get it to work. I don't know how to handle this kid at all. How am I going to survive a dozen more years with him, let alone struggle through a single day?

*

Terrible, huh?

Those were my ill-equipped parenting skills, and that was my son. Screaming. Kicking. Punching. Biting. Throwing things. A scary thing at three or five or even ten. But worse if I'd let his symptoms fester until he was older and bigger, a teen.

Now you know why I'm writing this book. I *lived* the story I'm about to tell, so I know just how significant it is. I know how monstrous the battles were. I know how lonely it felt to fight them. And I sense there's a tattered battalion of parents and guardians out there, crawling through the muck and minefields each day, living it, too.

Did your heart shudder as I said those words? Then, yes, I think this book's for you. Do you have a child who's violent and cruel and sucking the life from your very lungs? Then hear me now. There's hope. There is. And I'm going to show you what worked for us.

Or, wait. Maybe you don't have a child like the one I've described, and you've never seen one in public before. When you do (and you will), I beg you. Remember one simple thing. When you see a child who's screaming and smacking the only warm body who's trying to help. Please. Extend that stunned and weary parent and their monstrous child some grace. Don't stare. Don't whisper how awful he is. Move on. Say a prayer.

Or, perhaps, if the moment seems right, lean closer to that frazzled adult and whisper, "It's tough, but you're so doing great. Hang in there, okay?"

You might just give them the strength they need to get through a couple more hours in the fiercest fight of their lives.

But let's back up before we go on, if that's okay. Before I explain what's wrong with my son and what we did to set him free, there's something I want to show you first. I want you to see how very unprepared I was to have such a monstrous kid, and how desperately I wanted him, too.

Chapter 2

Grieving the Baby I Didn't Get

I lie on my side on the nursery floor, with Konner's body curled inside me, knowing how perfect my baby will be. I stare up at the empty crib, so white, unblemished and empty right now, and I'm flushed and bubbling with nervous excitement. I'm due in another two days. Two days!

Derrick tromps up the steps and stops in the doorway behind me. "There's a big stuffed chair you can sit in, you know."

"Funny." I pull myself up to sit, ignoring the way the rug fibers poke at my fleshy thighs.

He walks in the room and squats behind me. He's still in his suit, though his jacket hangs on the doorknob now.

It's over a hundred degrees outside, but the A/C feels good on my arms and legs. I'll sit in the chair soon enough, I think. To nurse my child. To rock him to sleep. How do I explain I *have* to be here, down here on the rug, looking *up* at the crib our son is going to be sleeping in soon?

"Two days," he says. "So hard to believe."

I tilt back my head to look at him, so his face is upside-down to me. "Two days too long."

His gentle eyes flicker with specks of gold, and he winks at me. My big strong man.

I blow up my cheeks and cross my eyes. Like a walrus, I'm sure. "All this waiting is awful. It's killing me."

He squeezes my shoulders and starts to knead.

"Mmm," I say. I'm huge and stretched. Everything aches.

He leans in close, next to my ear. "Do me a favor." I can almost sense Derrick wink behind me. "Go into labor tonight, will you? I'd like the day off."

I laugh. "I'll guess. Grumpy new boss?"

For the last two years, Derrick's worked as the head of information security at a global call center business. Unfortunately, his company is going through a merger, a fact we hope is not going to mean layoffs soon. Even though I make a good salary.

"Yeah, well," Derrick says. "I'm sure he'll be fine,"

"In a couple of years when you break him in."

He snorts at that and uses his knuckles to dig in deep.

I moan and let my eyes droop, relaxed. From under my lids I can see the smooth green sheet I've stretched over the baby's mattress. It's perfect, ready, waiting for *him*.

Derrick wraps his arms around me. They're bulky and hard from working outside, shoveling mulch, and from drumming downstairs in the basement at night. I've always been amazed at how many things he's really good at.

"What are you going to do?" he says. "After the baby comes, I mean?"

"Work." I laugh. I'm a business writer at IBM, a job I plan to return to after my three good months of maternity. I can work from home. Why wouldn't I? I'm proud of my work. Though Derrick's said he'd support me if I wanted to stay home instead. . He's the sweetest, I know it, but there's no room in my head for something like that. I'm a writer. I write. And now I'm having a baby, too.

"Before that," he says. "Before you go back." The vent's pumping out frosty air, which means Derrick turned the temperature down. He hates the heat.

I shiver against him. "Write, I guess." I've dreamt of writing a book for years, though writing is hard since I write for work. It drains my creative energy. "I'd love to finish a chapter or two." I can write while the baby naps, I think, because, of course, I assume it's going to nap.

"Maybe you can bring him to see me one day," Derrick says. "Have lunch with me."

"As soon as they tell me it's safe to expose him to all the germs out there, we will." My mind lights up and I think of all the places we'll go, the baby and me. "And then we're going to go *everywhere*." Trips to the zoo and outings with friends and those cool mommy-and-me swimming lessons. Things I've been dreaming of for years now.

Two years to be exact. And two rounds of in vitro fertilization just to be sitting where we are right now.

Our baby, Konner, is the sweet and miraculous answer to all our desperate prayers. Now, I can barely wait to hold him. And love him like crazy. And see the way he smiles at me for the very first time.

A baby who loves me, that's all I want. And a little time left to write if I can.

But life has a way of changing our plans, doesn't it? No matter how many things we give up to live the life we've been dreaming of, it never quite happens the way we think.

*

I moan and twist. I'm curled on my side, around my belly, squeezing the cold metal bed rail. I've labored for nearly thirteen hours and I'm not done yet.

"That's it, baby." Derrick is kneading my lower back. "You're doing so great."

I grit my teeth and pant my way through the grueling contraction. As soon as it's done, I slip into an exhausted sleep, made deep and strange, almost nightmarish, by the epidural that's taking a little edge off the pain. *Little* being the operative word.

A spasm yanks me out of my dream, just as hot and excruciating as the last contraction was.

"One more, Kristal," the doctor says. She's young and compact with a sunny voice. "I can see his head."

And then, with a scream and a harrowing push, he's finally out.

A soft and fluttery cry fills the delivery room. I close my eyes, trying to breathe, and listen to the sound of our baby's cries.

Konner's cries.

The doctor lays him down on my chest with his head to the side, and I place a shaky hand on his back. He's heavy, lying on top of me. Almost ten pounds I think I heard somebody say. Konner, I open my mouth to say, but I feel too weak to say it out loud. I try to focus my blurry eyes on his smushed red face, but my stomach is twisting sourly and a staticky rushing sound builds in my ears.

I mumble so soft I'm sure nobody else can hear. "Passing out."

As soon as I say it, a frantic dinging fills the small delivery room. It's the heart rate monitor spazzing out. And the baby is suddenly gone from my chest.

"Kristal?" My doctor leans over me. "Your placenta's not detaching, honey. It's not coming out. You're hemorrhaging." Little do I know, I've already lost two liters of blood. As much as you'd find in a large two-liter soda bottle. She looks across the bed at Derrick. "We're going to have to operate, to take it out."

He touches my hand and says something sweet I can't take in. Then they roll me swiftly into the hall, the wind of cool sterilized air washing over my face.

The next thing I know I'm slumped in bed in my hospital room, so swollen I can barely open my eyes. Derrick stands at the window nearby, the light glowing around his strong and shadowy frame. His arms are bent. Is he holding him?

"Derrick?" I say through the phlegm in my throat.

"Hey, you're awake." He turns, smiling, holding the baby. "How are you feeling?"

I try to swallow but my throat's too dry. "Beat." It's a condition I won't grow out of anytime soon.

He brings our baby over to me. "He's been missing his mama."

My eyes water and burn with tears. I lift my hands. And he helps me settle Konner in the crook of my left arm. I tilt down my head to look at him. And he's perfect, I see. So beautiful. He's muscular, strong, and I slip my finger into his hand. He squeezes it hard and opens his eyes. Those dark milky-blue newborn eyes. Eyes that seem to be looking for me. "Hello, sweet little Konner," I say.

I glance at Derrick. "So, hey, I guess you got the day off."

He laughs. "I did." He sits in the chair next to me, slumped. "A little more stressful than I thought it would be."

I manage a smile. "Sorry about that. If I scared you, I mean." I realize now how tired he looks, the way his face tugs around his eyes.

"They nearly took your uterus out." He shakes his head.

"But they didn't," I say. Which means I can still get pregnant again. Still, it's scary to know how close I was to becoming sterile, when I've dreamed of having three or four kids.

I look at Konner. My calm, quiet and watchful son. For a few more blissful hours, that is.

After that, the fussy and monstrous baby I really gave birth to will open its eyes and stay, for good. As if the labor and delivery I've endured are omens of all that's coming. And soon.

*

I walk downstairs, cradling Konner. He's heavy, so heavy for two months old. My arms ache and tremble from having to rock him to sleep. But he's sleeping now.

23

Something I hope will continue for more than a few minutes this time.

It's something I'm sure will get better soon. The crying, that is. And the lack of sleep. But, of course, it won't. If I knew that then, would I have done anything differently? Would I still have made the decision I made?

Ahead, through the narrow sidelights flanking our plum-colored door, the sky is a cool and washed-out white, the color of an early November sky, and the tall skinny pines that surround the houses across the street look sharp and gray against the white.

At the bottom of the steps I make a quick left and step into my open office. It's carpeted, spacious, with a wall of solid wood shelves and a desk. On top of that desk is a bulky black monitor, a monitor our cats Mischief and Mayhem love to sprawl out on whenever I'm working, due to the heat it pumps out on top.

I look at the desk, at the drawers filled with files, at the laptop that's closed and waiting for me, a laptop I take when I travel for work. And I think, how will I travel now? When I have a baby to think of, too? How will I do all the work I usually do in a day when I know my baby is in somebody's arms looking for me, and, not only that, when I'm looking for him?

Behind me, across from my desk, is a sleeper sofa I bought on my own for my first apartment. It's a huge stuffed piece, the frothy color of almond milk, and the arms are covered with these little pulls where our kittens once sharpened their kitten claws before I could teach them to use the post.

I sit on the couch and let out a soft exhausted sigh. I'm achy all over and it's good to sit. No. It feels like major relief. I spend a huge chunk of my day walking around with

Konner. If I don't, he constantly fusses or cries, and then I'm back up on my feet again.

My eyes go down to Konner's face. It's full and flushed against my chest and he works his little jaw as he sleeps. Pale hairs shimmer across his scalp and I stop myself from running my hand over them and waking him up. He's gorgeous, of course. Perfect in every way but three. Sleeping and eating and riding in cars (where he screams and screams like a leering beast is sitting there crouched on his little lap). Three things I always thought babies loved.

He's big for a baby. Ten pounds at birth and double that now. And he eats so much I need to supplement my milk with premade formula. Not milk-based, mind you. He spewed that out. And by spewed I mean *projectile* spewed. And he can't tolerate soy either. It makes him gassy and constipated, much fussier than he usually is. No, the formula I buy is special and allergen-free. Pricey. But he keeps it down, though he fusses as if he's not eating enough. Hopefully that changes when I'm able to incorporate some solid foods into his diet.

It *has* to, right?

I look at my desk. I love my job. And I love the people I work with, too. It's tough, challenging, fulfilling work. I write and oversee the materials our sales force needs to sell certain IBM servers to customers. And, before I left on maternity leave, I was overseeing the sales force's intranet site. I can't imagine doing anything else.

Except writing a book, of course. But that doesn't sound very practical now.

Konner makes smacking sounds with his mouth. Hungry sounds. And he's only been sleeping for a few minutes. I try to be as still as possible, to avoid waking him up again.

Still, I can't imagine putting him into somebody else's arms each day. I try to. I do. I imagine handing him over to the woman with wide blue sparkling eyes who lives down the street. She's agreed to watch him when I go back, but the idea of putting him in her arms and turning away makes me feel tense.

He's mine, I think. There's a possessiveness to it.

I shake my head. "I can't," I say in a whisper. "I can't." I can't give him up. And I realize I'm going to have to make a call. To Derrick, of course. Followed by calls to my manager, and the warm cheery woman down the street, too. To apologize and tell them I've changed my mind.

I've decided to stay home with my baby full time.

*

He's screaming again, these wet ragged cries that drag me out of a heavy sleep. He's five months old and hungry again. And he barely sleeps. I struggle my way out of bed in the dark and stumble across the hall to the glow of the nursery nightlight shaped like a lamb. His cries are quick and desperate now, and I lift him out of his perfect white crib and cradle him against me until he calms down.

I change his diaper as fast as I can, then I sit to nurse in the rocking chair I've come to dread. I live in that chair. At night in the dark. In a strange, semi-delusional state that reminds me of the labor I endured the night before Konner was born.

After he's finished, he's fussing again and I walk him around. But as soon as I stop moving around, he's crying again. Finally, his eyes look heavy. They close. And I lay him down on his back again. He spreads his arms so they're up by his head and I watch his eyes open and close a few times, before finally staying closed long enough that I turn for the hall.

I stumble back down the hall to bed.

An hour later, he's screaming again. It's a cycle we go through all day and all night. A cycle that often drives me to weep. A terribly unfortunate fact for me.

Because I gave my notice two months ago. And now I have nothing. Just screaming. Just this.

Chapter 3

Is This All There Is?

Konner, 3, and Brennig, 2, hugging, 2005

I push the rattling shopping cart over the pavement, weary, annoyed, wanting only to survive the day. *Survive* is a fitting word for it, too, though I don't know it yet. The air is thick and heavy with heat, and Konner, my oldest, who's two now, toddles beside me and twists and whines and tries to yank his hand out of mine.

I've suffered through nearly two years of this. Screaming, whining, biting, you name it. And we're well past the point of it wearing me out.

"No, Mama!" he cries. "Leggo!"

But, of course, I'm the mom. Despite how exhausted he's making me, I don't *leggo*. We're walking through a busy parking lot, with people and cars, most of which seem to be leaving now. And it's hard to hang onto Konner's hand while pushing a cart with his baby brother sitting up high in the metal seat.

By the time we reach the electric door, my shirt is damp.

The door snaps open ahead of us and a blast of frosty air hits us. I sigh and let Konner's hand go, and he runs ahead.

I stop at the fresh-picked corn stand and strip some ears of their tough green sleeves, peering at Konner now and then. One by one, I drop them into a plastic bag. Konner loves corn, thankfully. It's one of the few foods he'll eat without throwing a fit.

"Stay close," I say.

He squeals and runs a circle around the apples case.

Meanwhile, the baby, Brennig, nine months, looks grumpy and flushed in his metal perch, unhappy I've strapped him in again after waking him up in the parking lot. He tries to lift the flimsy strap that holds him in.

I press him down in the seat again. "Sit still, baby. For Mama. Please." To say my body feels heavy, exhausted, is an understatement. Konner hasn't napped since Brennig was born, ten months ago. And Brennig has just started to walk.

I'm lost, in a way. No job and no time to write at all. And I don't enjoy mothering in the least anymore. Did I ever? I think. Konner's constant tantrums make it hard to enjoy my little one, too.

I trudge through the store as fast as my tired legs will go, while Konner snatches down crackers and boxes of juice, and sugary cereals. One at a time, I shelve them again. After the fourth or fifth time I do it, Konner drops to the floor and screams.

Brennig pops up in the seat again. I force him to sit. The belt is long and ridiculously loose. "Sit down, sweetie."

Two women with carts pause, looking displeased with me, as Konner shrieks and writhes on the floor.

Helpful, I think. They stare as if I've made him this way by spoiling him. And that's the way they're looking at me. I crouch beside his squirming form, wishing only for rest, some sleep.

"Konner." I struggle him up to his feet. "Stop screaming. Be good. If you still want a treat when we're done, okay?"

He grunts.

Thank God. And he toddles off with cobwebs of snot stretched from his nose to his plump red cheek. At the end of an aisle, he grabs a bag of potato chips. He crinkles it loudly between his hands.

I sigh. "No chips." I put them back.

By time we reach the coolers of meat, I'm jittery, ready to leave, go home. Luckily, the area's empty for now. Nobody here to glare at me. And the only thing left I need is meat.

Across from the coolers is a big display of chocolate chip cookies.

Great, I think. Why did they have to put cookies there?

"Cookies!" my monster screams. "Wight now!" He stomps in a circle around the cart, flapping his arms like chicken wings.

I'd probably laugh if I weren't so tired. And horrified. I'm a traditionalist as a parent, I guess, expecting my children to be kind and respectful. And helpful, too. Even at two. But Konner is barely teachable.

"Cookies!" he screams, over and over.

I grab his wrist and squeeze it. "Stop it. Stop it right now."

He frowns at me with a pooched red face.

"Last warning. Got it?" I let him go.

36

He stomps away and grabs a box of cookies down. "Cookies! Wight now!"

I sigh. I'm done. "No treats, Konner. I warned you, okay? That's not behaving."

"No!" He jumps up and down in his boots. "No, no, no!" And he clomps toward me and waves a box of cookies at me.

"I said, no treat." I step around him to pick up a pack of New York strips and some chicken breasts. Then I hear some soft scuffling sounds and a grunt followed by a ragged breath.

My stomach does a slippery flop. Brennig! I think. I spin around.

A woman holds Brennig upside down, around the ankle, his fingers brushing the tiled floor and his legs open like a pair scissors.

I cover my mouth, in total shock at the way she's caught him. Then I drop the meat with a wet slap and rush to my son. "Thank you," I say, lifting him out of the woman's hand. "Oh my, God, thank you. Thank you so much."

I cradle him gently against my chest, unable to breathe after what I've seen.

He starts to cry, softly at first, then reddens, goes loud. I smooth the downy hair on his head. The head that nearly struck the tiles. "Shhhh," I say. I kiss him all over his fuzzy head. "It's okay. You're fine." But it isn't fine. I almost lost my baby.

I did.

Konner is holding my leg, tugging, and whining now.

"Hang on," I say.

I peer around and look for the woman, wanting to thank her one more time, but there's no one in sight. Not a single other customer, in fact.

"Come on, Konner." With Brennig balanced against my hip, I roll the cart to the other aisles, peering down one at a time. But the woman's gone. She's nowhere in sight. I stop and stare at the canned goods aisle, where a mom with three tiny and docile kids, inspects an oversized can of soup, and I realize I can't shake it. The hand that caught my son.

I feel my entire body slump, barely able to believe what happened. That Brennig somehow pulled off the strap and pushed up onto his wobbly feet and dove from the cart. What are the chances she'd be right there when he took that dive?

She's an angel, I think. That's what she is. She saved his life.

I glance down at Konner who's standing, unusually quiet, beside me, and sucking his thumb. Seriously? Now? He's calm for me *now*?

It was all my fault. I know that, of course. I wasn't paying attention to Brennig. My fault. But I worry about the way that Konner's increasingly monstrous behavior is always distracting me. My eyes are constantly focused on him. And away from his brother. A brother who whimpers against me.

Alive.

*

It's January, the following year. Gloomy and frigid. The day of my failed intervention. I guide our big blue SUV onto a quiet two-lane road, surrounded by trees on either side. The trunks are stripped of their vivid costumes and shivering in their lizard skins.

The monster is three. Smart. Husky. And killer-cute in his yellow work boots. He sits in his booster seat right behind me while Brennig plays with his hands behind the passenger seat.

"Okay, guys," I say. "We're stopping at Mimi's to drop off a book, then I have to go to the grocery store." I glance in the rearview mirror. At Konner. "You hear that, bud? We don't have time to stop in today. And Mimi has a headache anyway."

I think about that, then say, "If you're good, we'll get a treat at the store, okay?" Positive reinforcement, I guess. Though it rarely works. Northing much works.

Konner nods, up-down, up-down, to a beat that matches the feet he's kicking against the seat. *Thump-thump, thump-thump, thump-thump, thump-thump.*

"Thoppih, Konnoh," Brennig says in a heavy lisp. *Stop it, Konner.*

"Please," I say. "Stop kicking the seat."

Thump-thump. Thump-thump.

I roll my eyes. Of course, he doesn't listen to me. He never does. And I'll scream if I have to keep listening to that. It's not just the boots, it's the constant parade of noises he makes. Crying, screaming, yelling, kicking, thumping, smacking his toys together, and the rushed and manic way he talks.

"Music?" I say, speaking up, and I touch the circular radio dial, hoping a minor distraction will help.

"CD 3, number 6!" Konner spits it out fast to beat out his brother from choosing one first. I glance in the rearview mirror again. At his fat flushed cheeks, grinning for once, and his huge chocolatey eyes that sparkle.

I shake my head. Unhappy that he always has to be first, but also amazed. There are six CDs in the dashboard player. And it never ceases to amaze me how he's memorized every single song and CD by number. There have to be eighty songs at least. "You're crazy smart, you know that, kiddo?"

Then I glance around and wink at Brennig. "You and your brother both, my love."

Brennig smashes his lips together like he's holding in some secretive laugh. It's a smile I love. I start to relax.

Ten minutes later, I pull up to my parent's house, a cute buttery colored Cape Cod with a green front door. The heavy thump of the band Disciple fills the truck. It'll keep them entertained for a minute. I hope.

"Where's Kaila?" says Konner.

"At school." I push out the door. And the cold air slaps me hard in the face.

"Wait, Mama!" Konner says.

"Just a minute, Konner." I'm tired of him always controlling me. "I'll be right back." And I close the door with a final thump.

With the car running, I crunch ten feet through salt to the door. I pull out the clear outer door and knock. Then I push it in. "Mom?"

Behind me comes a loud but muffled scream I'd know if thirty kids screamed at the same time.

"Unbelievable!" I growl. I drop the book on the dense brown rug. "Mom! I'm leaving the book right here! I have to go!"

"Kristal?" she calls from the back of the house.

"Konner's throwing a fit again!" And I hurry back to the SUV.

I yank out his door. "What's going on?"

Brennig is holding his ears and baring his teeth, in pain.

Konner is smeared with snot and tears. "I want Kaila to hear this song!" Kaila. His sweet and doting eight-year-old cousin.

"Kaila's not here. Remember?" I say.

He blinks.

"She's at school."

He throws back his head, mouth wide, and wails.

And there goes my afternoon. No store.

"Kristal?"

I turn.

My mom stands at the door in her dark glasses, clutching her robe around her neck. "Can I do anything?"

I shake my head. It's so loud, I can't talk. With a wave, I hop in and slam the door.

"Mimi!" he screams. "Mimi! Help!"

In the rearview mirror, his arms are extended, reaching for my mom.

First Kaila, now her. I'm not about to give in to his screams.

I put the truck into reverse and back onto the quiet street. Quiet, that is, except for the piercing screams in our car. I need to start keeping some earplugs handy.

When we reach the wider two-lane road, I take a right, my ears pounding, shoulders hunched. "Konner!" I say. "Stop screaming! Enough!"

Then Brennig lets out a panicky cry.

I look around, panicked myself. What do I do? There isn't a shoulder along the road, so I can't pull off. Do I drive all the way home like this?

I glimpse a long low building ahead, a fire station, and something connects. Something a woman said at church two weekends ago. Something she did when her own young daughter wouldn't behave.

I grit my teeth, since I'm not really sure it's a good idea, but I have to do *something*. Or else I'll join in with the screaming soon.

At the last minute, I turn the wheel, going faster than I should, I guess, considering all the potholes here. The car bounces into the lot, jarring my teeth, and the screams diminish. Thank God for that. The lot is empty. There isn't a single car, so I stop. To the right is the station's entrance, a stoop with a big metal door.

I rest my arm on the back of my seat and half turn.

And that's when the proverbial mud hits the fan, splattering all over my parenting skills: a mother beaten by her own child in the parking lot.

My arms hurt where my three-year-old son has pummeled me, and I fear the monster that sits in his seat. Afraid it's going to hit me again.

"You're going right to your room!" I say.

He glares at me.

"If you scream, we're going to come back. Understand?" For the moment, I don't even care what'll happen if I don't follow through and come back again. I want to get home and call my husband. Who'll hopefully know what I'm supposed to do.

I slink into my bucket seat like a beaten dog and peer at Brennig. He's glassy-eyed, stunned, and he stares out at the empty building. I know how he feels.

I put the SUV into drive. And as soon as I pull back

onto the road, I hear *thump-thump, thump-thump, thump-*

thump.

It's the sound of Konner's boots again.

And I think, *What's wrong with this awful kid? And*

why does it feel like it's all my fault?

*

The waiting room is large but sparsely populated, a

relief to me since I usually have to scoop up my children

and run out of places when the Konner alarm starts going

off. On the floor, about twenty feet away from me, a wiry

man in a navy suit paces back and forth in front of Konner,

still 3, who's banging some plastic blocks together.

It's been a few months since that botched

intervention in the parking lot. But something is very

wrong with my son. He screams all the time and he's

becoming increasingly physical, too. I just need to know what's wrong with him. To know what to do. Because Derrick doesn't think there's anything wrong. He just thinks Konner's a strong-willed child who needs a bit of a heavy hand.

But that isn't what I am sensing at all. I know my child is monstrous and mean, and constantly trying to manipulate me. And I need to know why. What's wrong with him? I need a little hope there's something I can do to make things better. For me. As well as our family.

I watch the man, a developmental pediatrician, and try to figure out what he's doing with Konner, since he's not interacting much with my son. I watch from my seat with an arm around Brennig who's on my lap. He's almost two and I've been reading him a small hard-cover book about a barn and the animals who live in it.

A happy barn. And I think, do those families exist in the world? Happy families where everyone usually gets along?

Brennig grabs a cardboard page and turns it as soon as I finish reading. He knows this book. It's a favorite of his. But my eyes go down to the words then up to the doctor again.

The man was recommended by a friend of mine, and it took us an hour-and-a-half to get here. I'm desperate, I think. So desperate to have an answer. Something.

He squats down and says something to Konner, something I can't hear from my chair, and Konner makes an angry face. He whips the blocks at the wall where they thunk and then fall to the thin carpeted floor.

The doctor nods, says a few more words, then he heads my way. He waves. "Can we talk in my office?" He points to a room behind my shoulder. "As soon as you've got the kids together."

I tense, wondering how I'm going to wrangle two kids, well, Konner, and meet him there. "Okay. I'll try."

I glance around at the office and chairs sitting behind me, then I look at Konner. He's plodding toward me. Thank goodness. That's actually a huge relief. I don't have to yank him away from the blocks.

I put Brennig down, who starts to cry, then I take his hand. "We'll finish the book at home, okay?" Then I hook the diaper bag over my shoulder and hold a hand out for Konner to take. He slaps it, hard, then shoves it away.

I give him a tired, disgusted look. "Konner," I say and I point to the room. "The doctor needs us to go in there."

He grunts. A 'no.' "Go home," he says.

I nod. "Yes. And I'll let you watch a DVD in the car, too, if you come into the office with me. Just a few minutes. And then we'll go."

I reach for him and he slaps me again. After a scream and a little more coaxing, he finally toddles into the room. He hops on a chair and swings his legs, so the rubbery seat constantly squeaks, and I hand him a tiny lollipop. To keep him quiet. Brennig whimpers and reaches for me. He always gets everything last, I'm afraid, since his brother constantly ticks like a bomb. I unwrap another lollipop and hand it to Brennig. Then I sit in a chair, with Brennig standing on the floor beside me, swaying a bit, so tired he looks like he's going to pass out. But not crying yet, fortunately.

The doctor closes the door and settles behind his desk.

"So what do you think?" I ask. "Can you tell?" What's wrong with my child?

He folds his arms on top of his desk and nods at Konner vigorously. "I see what you mean. He's willful and easily angered, too. I've seen this in a lot of children of late. It's called Oppositional Defiant Disorder. Or ODD. Great acronym, huh? Some kids just have that defiant sort of temperament. They're hard to work with."

Brennig lays a hand on top of my wrist. It's hot. Sticky. I shake my head, feeling pulled by the kids, unable to think of all the questions I'd like to ask. "So what does that mean?"

"More work for you. He'll make your job more challenging."

He already does. "What can I do?"

"Take some parenting classes, I'd say."

"What kind?" I ask, since I'd already taken one at church, and I'd read more books than I knew how to count.

"On parenting a tough, oppositional kid."

"That's it?" I say. So I'm getting no help at all from this.

Konner slides down and starts to tug at my free arm. "Come on, Mama. Come on. Less go."

The doctor moves papers around on his desk. "It's tough, I know. It'll take some time to know the best way to handle him. But that's really all you can do for now. Besides taking some time for yourself."

Time? What time?

I stare at him, drained. Three hours of driving, an hour of waiting, five minutes of observation time, and that's all I get. Take a class on the best way to handle my child. A child who screams and hits non-stop. But I can't really put all those thoughts into words with a child tugging at each of my arms.

I stand. "Okay. Well, thank you, doctor." What else can I say? Then Konner yanks me out of the office, all the way out to the parking lot.

I open his door so he can climb in.

He holds up a hand. "Lollipop."

"Apple," I say. I have healthier snacks inside the car.

He shows me his fist. "Lollipop!"

"I'm sorry, no. Not talking like that." I'm a pretty strict mother, usually. But only because Konner responds exactly like this. I have no clue what else would work better with him. The tactics listed in a book on parenting strong-willed kids didn't work with him. So the two of us battle for control all day. Is every single second of every single day as awful as the next? Well, no. Not always. But usually, yeah.

We have moments of sweet bright happy smiles. Occasionally. But I feel the tension running under it all, and I'm always so stressed, always holding my breath.

He bares his teeth and growls at me. And I know exactly what happens next. I know the screaming starts up again. And I know Brennig and I are going to be imprisoned by that screaming all the way home.

*

Alone, I think. Alone at last. I sit at my desk in the quiet house and breathe the relief of being alone, a breath that's matched by the sound of the A/C vent overhead. It's sultry outside, though it's almost November. A fact I love. But not quite as much as I love being free of the kids today.

Scratch that.

I really mean Konner-free.

He's five and he's handling Kindergarten, but his tantrums at home are worse than ever. For now, I'm totally free of all that.

I place my fingers on the keyboard and type. I manage to write an entire page of the novel I've been working on before the phone rings.

I glance at the phone. Oh no. Not again. I've been getting calls about Konner's behavior. But not from the school. Not once, in fact. Somehow, he's able to hold it together for half a day. But he's bussed to daycare twice a week after school to give me a break, and that's where I'm getting the calls from. Calls to come pick Konner up.

I reach for the phone and look at the time. It's early. Eleven. He's still at school. But the number is one I don't recognize. Maybe a telemarketer. But I've stupidly pushed the button. "Hello?"

"Oh, great!" says the woman. Cheery, relieved. "Is this Kristal?"

"Yes?"

"We've been trying to get a hold of you."

We? I think. Telemarketer. How long should I wait until I hang up?

"You wrote this wonderful story, 'Unplugged.'"

There's a lump in my throat. 'Unplugged'? I think. She's read 'Unplugged.' And I sit up straight. It's set in the future, and it follows the mother of a baby who cries, a mother who's forced to unplug from her job in the neural net just to deal with the screaming. Sound familiar? "Yes?"

"I'm pleased to tell you it's won second place in our annual contest. Ahead of 15,000 other entries!"

My chest expands. I can barely breathe. Is this happening? "Really?"

"Yes!" she says. "And it comes with a check!"

I stand, pulsing with energy. I can write! I think. I can actually write. And, better than that, I'm going to get paid!

*

Thirty minutes later, I'm floating, in shock, when I push through the heat into the boys' daycare center. I sign the boys out in the register and smile at the woman with the long dark hair who sits at the desk. Miss Jennifer.

Her face doesn't gleam like it usually does, but I'm too distracted to think it might somehow apply to me.

"Good day?" she says.

The entire staff knows I'm trying to write while the boys are here, so they'll often ask what I'm working on. Only this time I actually have some decent news. "One of my stories won second place in a national contest!"

Her mouth makes a round little O, surprised. "Your boys are going to be proud of their mama."

Gosh, I hadn't thought about that.

"Miss Ellen asked to see you," she says. "Did she call you at home?"

"No." I frown. "Are the boys okay?" I feel a sour twist in my twist. A Konner twist.

"Oh," she says, sounding surprised. "No, they're fine. She just needed to see you." She extricates herself from her desk. "Stay here. I'll run and get her."

I watch her hurry down the long hall.

Miss Ellen is Konner's teacher, of course. She's usually the one who calls me at home. In a moment, I see her wavy red hair poke from a doorway. No turn of the head. No wave.

Not good.

Miss Jennifer takes her place and doesn't come out again. A moment later, Miss Ellen is plodding her way toward me. She's a big woman with a big voice and a big heart, and she finally waves, but she doesn't smile.

I slump. What did he do? Oh no.

She nods for me to follow her through the small front office, into the back. The owner's office. She closes the door and sits on the desk. She tries to smile and can't. She sighs. "Konner used a pencil as a weapon today."

A weapon. "He what?"

"He scratched a boy hard. Leaving these marks." She tries to describe their size and shape with her fingertips, but finally gives up.

I shake my head, unable to wrap my head around it. "Why?" I say. "Why did he do it?"

She lets out a weary breath. "I'm afraid the boy said he's mean. That nobody likes him." She lifts her hands. "He shouldn't have said it, I know. I'm sorry."

"Me too," I say, remembering the wiry guy in the suit we saw in the summer. Mr. ODD. It's a label that says my kid is cruel and difficult. But it doesn't get to the *root* of the problem. The root of the rage he carries around. And the things we can do to actually fix it. Something's wrong. Extremely wrong. But part of me doesn't want to know how wrong it actually is.

Miss Ellen's face looks stormy, conflicted. A look I've started to recognize. We've gotten to be friends the last few months. It's a shame, since I know what's coming next.

Ten minutes later, I walk into the baking heat with my tiny boys trailing behind me. And I can't help it. I hate the monster I call my son.

It screams. It bites. It claws. It hits. It shreds an entire room to ribbons. And it controls the movements of any adult who crosses its path. Especially me. And it's stolen all the joy out of my writing win.

That monster has now been kicked out of daycare. At five years old.

It looks so normal on the outside. I know. It looks like my son. But it's *not* my son. Where is he? I think. Where is my son?

Chapter 4

A Glimmer of Hope

Konner in his 1st Grade School Photo, 2008

It's hard to watch Derrick packing to leave on another trip. I'm panicked inside. Scared of being left with the monster I feel like I'm raising alone. Could I beg Derrick to stay home this time? Just for this week? But, no, I can't stand to do that to him. So I keep myself stiff and dry-eyed instead. For Derric's sake. For the boys' as well.

In the kitchen, I watch Derrick kneel on the tiles to hug Konner and say goodbye to him. Before Derrick can touch him, though, Konner ducks out from under his hands.

Konner yells "Bye!" before running out. And a moment later, I hear the squeal of his sneakers hitting the wooden treads as he runs upstairs to his room.

It's so hard to talk to Konner about Derrick's traveling. Konner acts so indifferent about it on the one hand. Like he doesn't care. Then he throws a tantrum as soon as Derrick's out the door.

"Where are you going?" Brennig says in his sweet high voice. He's 4 years old and he's barely able to hold in his tears.

Derrick places a hand on his arm. "On a trip for work. I'm sorry, bud. But we'll go out for donuts on Saturday morning like we usually do. As long as you guys are good for Mama." Or, as long as Brennig is good for Mama. Because Konner usually misses out.

Tears are sliding down Brennig's face and his stormy blue eyes are so big and sad it's hard to look straight into them. "But why?" he says. "Do you need alone time away from us. Is that why you leave?"

A tear slips out of my eye and I quickly swipe it away.

"Away from *you*?" Derrick pulls him into a hug. "Not a chance. No way. I'd rather be here with you. But I can't. I have to go to Detroit. Because it's my job, okay?" He pulls back with a look of concern. "Could you do me a favor?"

Brennig nods.

"Give your mom a big hug for me when I'm gone?"

My stomach shudders and I struggle against the pressure of tears that have built in my eyes. I cover my lips with both of my hands.

Brennig peers up with his watery eyes and I lower my hands to smile at him as best I can. I pull him in close as Derrick leans in to kiss my mouth. His lips are warm and dry against mine and I lay my hand on his smooth-shaven cheek, brushing the edge of his goatee.

"I love you," he says, and his eyes narrow with worry.

I smile. It's the calmest smile I can muster up. Then I kiss him again, trying to hold on to a piece of him to keep while he's gone. "I love you, too. Have a safe flight."

He bends over to grab his bags, then steps outside into the garage. And that panicky feeling trembles through me as the garage door rumbles down and closes, leaving me utterly and completely alone.

*

The following morning, a warm fall day, I open the bathroom mirror and pull out a bright yellow tube of hair gel. The bus will arrive in ten more minutes. There isn't much time. But it's picture day, and Konner started first grade this year. It's hard to believe, he's six years old.

I squeeze a blob into my palm. While Derrick's away, I tiptoe around landmines all day. The kind that trip and my son explodes.

Brennig darts in, scoops some goop onto his finger, and scampers off.

"Thief!" I laugh. "Don't go too far. I drop you off next."

I lean out the bathroom and peer down our long rectangular kitchen. It's bright because of the recessed lights, while outside it's gray and threatening.

"Hey, Konner?" I say, bracing myself for a rude response.

He sits at the round kitchen table, marker in hand, and furiously draws circle after circle on a piece of grey construction paper. His entire arm moves with the pen.

"Can I gel your hair?"

He glances up. And he looks so cute in his blue polo and khaki shorts. Like a cherub minus the fluttering wings. If I didn't already know better, that is.

"Like Cara did when she cut your hair?"

His cheeks are puffy chipmunk cheeks. He frowns at me. A warning sign. But he doesn't say no. Just slides off the chair and lumbers toward me. Okay then, I think. I guess that's a yes.

He stands before me, arms crossed, in the cramped half bath. I hunch over him and work some gel into the fringe above his forehead. Then I smooth it back into his hair. Ten seconds at most. And it gives his hair the cutest swoop for picture day. So adorable. I straighten up.

His face is red, like he's holding his breath.

"What's wrong?" I say. "Do you want to see?" I take a step back from the sink to let him look in the mirror.

Instead, he lets out a furious shriek and smacks at the front of his hair with his hands. My stomach is tight. I'm afraid he's going to come after me next.

When I step back again, I bump the sink, with nowhere to go.

"Konner," I say in a low voice. "The bus is coming." It's a warning, I guess. To stop this before this goes too far.

He's panting hard, his hands fisted against his sides.

"Why did you do that?" I say.

71

He growls.

I raise my hands, surrendering, unsure what to do. Is he going to be able to go to school?

He stomps away and I trail after him through the kitchen and into the front entryway. Brennig peers in from the front room, eyes wide and frightened. I point to the stairs, giving him a clear escape route, and he sprints straight up.

I stand nearby, eyeing Konner, afraid of setting him off again. At the door, he grabs his backpack off the area rug and sticks an arm into each of the straps. Then he opens the door with a fist, walks out and slams the door hard. So hard the glass in the door and windows rattle, shocked.

Unable to bawl or giggle like some sort of lunatic, I bite my hand. Hard enough to hurt. Then I step outside onto the stoop. It's chilly and my arms prickle with gooseflesh. I hug myself, as much from the stress as the nip of cold.

Konner stands at the bottom of our long curving drive, rigid and quiet, facing the road.

I rub my thumb, where I feel the dented outline of teeth. Is he going to scream at the kids on the bus? Should I keep him home? What should I do?

But it's already been decided for me.

The bus rolls to a stop beside him, its lights flashing. It lets out a shrill squeal of brakes and opens its doors. Please, I think. Let everything go okay today.

It rolls away and I stare after it, sick with dread. When I go inside and close the door, there's none of that relief of having him gone.

"Brennig?" I call upstairs. "You okay?"

"I'm otay, Mama."

He still goes to daycare twice a week and, although I feel a bit guilty about it, I need the break more than I care to admit these days. "We'll leave in five."

"Otay," he says.

I'd normally smile at his sweet lisp, but I walk into the kitchen, tense. When l look at the table where Konner was sitting, I see the drawing he's left there.

And I pick it up.

It's a large continuous scribble of circles he drew on grey, starting off small at the bottom and widening out into huger circles up top. It makes a crude but telling picture.

A black tornado.

The sour dread in my belly twists. I have no idea what to do with this. With any of this.

Two hours later, the phone rings. It isn't the first time the school has called, and it won't be the last. But this time, it's worse. I actually expect it.

"Hello?" I say.

"Hi, Mrs. Johnson. It's Konner's teacher." It's a sing-song voice. "Mrs. Neer."

"Is anything wrong?"

"Actually…yes." A pause. "I'm sorry to tell you this. Konner pushed a little girl down, a classmate, at picture time."

Pushed, I think. This child will be the death of me. "Did he say why he did it?"

"He wanted to reach the front of the line before anyone else."

I massage my temple, so hard it hurts. "I don't understand why he's doing these things." This isn't typical boy behavior. I know that at least. Brennig's so sweet and calm and helpful. So unlike his brother. Not that I can take credit for that. He's been that way since the day the doctor handed him over to me in the hospital.

"Can you come pick him up?"

"Of course," I say.

"Maybe we could chat. Before you take him. The kids are about to head to lunch."

*

Ten minutes later, the teacher and I sit at a low round table, in a couple of miniature chairs that make me feel five years old.

Mrs. Neer smiles, a schoolgirl smile, under her swoop of long blond hair. Her eyes are full of hopes and dreams. Dreams I had a long time ago. "Thank you so much for coming," she says. "I'm worried about Konner."

I nod, frowning, out of my mind with worry, too. But I'm not about to let her see how out of control I feel. I've already seen the knowing looks of the other staff, and they aren't about to share what they know. Why won't someone give me some answers? What's wrong with my son? What should I do?

Or maybe they don't have a clue. Like me.

"Is everything okay at home, Mrs. Johnson?"

"Excuse me?" I say.

"Anything that might play a role in all this. Like the reason why Konner's so angry here." She cocks her head and her face is perfectly smooth, diplomatic. Even her bright red lipstick somehow looks practical.

"My husband travels a bit, that's all."

"I see," she says, but she still looks baffled. "Do you think Konner's upset about that?"

"Honestly?" I say. "I have no idea what makes him upset. He's always upset. He flew off the handle with me this morning when I gelled his hair. Why? I don't know. Why do you ask?"

She smooths her skirt where it covers her lap. "He's not making friends, I'm afraid. He screams when they try to help. Yesterday, a pencil rolled off his desk and onto the floor, and a little boy stooped to pick it up. Konner just started screaming at him."

I don't really know what to say to that. It's typical Konner.

"The parents are getting uncomfortable. They're telling their kids to stay away from him."

I blink. I feel stung, and somehow accused. Did I really need to know all that?

"What do you think we should do?" she says.

We? I'm feeling outnumbered, although there are only two of us sitting here. "We use a reward chart at home," I say. "With plastic stars. For his good behavior. If he earns enough stars, he can turn them in for a small prize. Is that something we can do here at school?"

Her face lights up. She looks delighted. "Wonderful. Yes." She turns and grabs some index cards from the desk behind her. "What if I give him a smiley sticker on the days he behaves, and a sad sticker on the days he doesn't? He can turn the card in to you for a prize, at home each day, and that way you can see how he's doing, too."

It's almost as if it's all her idea. "Sure." I nod. "We can do that. Great." So we're done here then.

I stand, grateful to stretch my legs, and I hook my purse over my shoulder.

She scribbles a note on one of the cards, then presses a sticker down with her thumb. She holds it high so I'll take it from her.

"Thanks," I say.

"Make sure you show it to Konner," she says. "And I'll tell him more when I see him tomorrow. But Mrs. Johnson."

"Yes?"

"If he hurts anybody else, he's going to be expelled, I'm afraid."

I stare at her. *Daycare.* That's all I think.

She stands and smooths her wrinkles out. "But I'm sure that won't happen."

She's not. But I am.

Which means I have to find someone who's actually seen this before. Who knows what this is. If that somebody even exists out there.

*

He screams and thumps on the other side of the office door.

I'm nervous, stiff, and I sit with Derrick on a bench in the small glassed entryway, waiting for Konner's shrink (I mean his psychiatrist), to evaluate him. Dr. De Hay. It's our second visit to the man so far. And he doesn't even take insurance.

Derrick puts a strong arm around me. "It's fine. Relax." He tips his smooth shaved head forward to look at me.

I give his goatee a playful tug. "For two-fifty an hour, yeah. It better be." But I'm also thinking about

Konner's behavior most of the time, and the fact he's always bubbling with magma, about to erupt. I know how much it scares me now, especially since he's gotten bigger. Bigger and stronger. And Derrick is constantly on the road.

"What do you think he'll find?" says Derrick.

I shake my head. "He better not tell me it's ODD. Or I'll clock him one."

He chuckles at that.

I hear the wooden scrape of a door. To our right, light spills from an open doorway, where the doctor stands. He gives us a wide self-assured smile beneath his brown and fluffy hair. "Mr. and Mrs. Johnson," he says, and he holds up a hand, inviting us in.

The office is large and relaxed, but also orderly. It's full of beautifully distressed barnwood furniture, including a large glass-topped desk, but my eyes go to the spot where

Konner kneels on the rug, quiet, intense, as he snaps together some lego blocks. A quiet I know won't last long.

"Please, have a seat." Dr. De Hay sits in a deep leather chair not far from Konner's spot on the floor, and Derrick and I sink into the other two chairs that face him.

"Let's get down to business. Shall we?" The doctor gives us another poised smile. "What we're looking at here is Asperger's. Do you know what that is?"

I glance at Derrick. "I've heard of it." It's an autism spectrum disorder. I frown. "It explains the outbursts?"

He spreads his hands. "It certainly does."

I peer at Derrick. What does he think?

He reaches over and squeezes my hand. *You wanted an answer.* His eyebrows go up. *Didn't you?*

I nod. I do. And I link my fingers into his. I just didn't expect to hear autism. And nothing else. I'd braced for a mental illness. Bipolar. *Something* to explain his raging moods.

The doctor clasps his hands together. "Konner's rigid when it comes to change and he spirals into tantrums a lot. He's fixated on legos here, and Aspy kids do tend to fixate. His inability to accept the word 'no' makes him fly into a rage as well. And his condition makes it hard to be compassionate, to socialize, to make any friends." He lifts a hand. "He's in his own world, as I like to say, and he wants to stay there."

I nod. That's true. All of that's true. And I worry about the friendship part. Of him being alone without any friends.

"I'd like to put him on an anti-convulsant," the doctor continues. "To help with his irritability. It's a medication that helps a lot of autistic kids."

My mind whirls with what he's just said, and what it will mean. My child is going to be on meds? "Can we think about it?"

"Of course," he says and he shows us out.

Back in the car, Konner kicks and screams. "Treat! Give me my treat! Right now!"

I try to ignore him. To ignore the behavior. "So, meds," I say, raising my voice.

Derrick looks troubled. "Meds," he agrees. His goatee moves with the sound of the word.

"I guess—" and I shake my head. "I guess if that's what he needs—" But I can't seem to finish my thought with the noise that he's making in back. I look around at Konner again, who's acting a lot like a toddler instead of a 6-year-old. I hold up a plastic bag and shake it. Inside are some cookies. "Stop screaming first."

"Treat!" screams Konner. "I want my treat!" The treat we promised for answering the doctor's questions tonight.

Derrick starts up the car. It roars to life around us. "I honestly don't know what he needs," he says.

Konner shrieks.

"Okay, no treat." I look around at Konner, so sick of his awful behavior. He's thrashing side to side in his seat and screaming so loud I nearly get out.

"Just go," I say. Just hurry. Get home. All I want is crawl into bed for a year and disappear. If only, I think. And I raise my voice. "But I'd still like to get a second opinion."

*

Days later, Konner raises his hand to answer a subtraction problem during class. When the teacher doesn't call on him, he screams and throws all the things in his desk at the other kids. Pencils. Papers. Erasers. Even his pencil case.

He's expelled, of course, and tucked away temporarily into an intensive day treatment school, while we work with a new psychiatrist to put him on meds. Oh, yeah, didn't I mention that? He can't go back to school until he's been stabilized. On medication. If something like that's even possible.

Normally the bus takes him to and from the facility, but today they've asked me to pick him up. Saying he's angry, too volatile, to ride the bus home.

I step from the car, wearing my longest, bulkiest coat. It's November, raw, and the sky's a hard and menacing blue. My breath feels frosty inside my lungs. I take a shallow breath in the cold and head for the door.

When I press the doorbell, a dark bored guard sits slumped in a tiny glass entry room. He buzzes me in. Like the place is a prison.

The guard, who's packing pepper spray, steps out of his booth to escort me. "This way," he says.

In the hallway, we pass two other guards who snicker about a clash with a kid. "Man, I took that kid down to the ground, ho boy," a big guy says. The other man snorts. Laughing about it. Just beautiful.

I can't believe it. My body cries out against this place, this child prison, but right now this place is our only option. All I can hope is they weren't talking about Konner.

The guard stops at the room and nods his head toward the door.

"Thanks," I say and I step inside. It's small and, despite the overhead lights, it's not well lit. Ten feet away, a man with a short black ponytail, a teacher I know as Mr. J, kneels besides Konner's desk.

Konner's slumped with his forehead down, and his hoodie covers the top of his head.

The man looks up with a tired smile.

"What happened?" I say.

Konner jerks up, out of his seat, and runs to me.

I spread my legs, since I see what's coming, and Konner barrels into me, hard. He gives me the tightest, fiercest hug. I hug him back and say, "Hey, baby," because that's what a mother is supposed to do. Even a mother as weary as me.

Mr. J stands. "He has a tough time transitioning, as we know, of course." He gestures down at Konner's desk. "Konner was working hard on math. He's a machine at getting his classwork done. But as soon as I said, 'It's time for gym,' he refused to go. I gave him a warning. No surprise. But he jumped from his desk and hit me here." He presses his hand to his diaphragm. "Knocked the air right out of me. We put him in one of the quiet rooms until he calmed down."

"Quiet rooms?" I look around, but I don't see another door in the class.

"Out in the hall."

Konner peers up from my stomach. His gaze is pleading with mine. "Can we go now, please? Can we please just go?"

I look over at Mr. J. "Can I see one first?"

"Sure." He walks out, into the hall.

I follow him, but Konner tugs me, slowing me down.

"That's enough," I say. "I need to see it. And then we can go."

Mr. J walks to the end of the hall. And stops. He points.

There's a door in the corner. The door is metal, painted a pale and ghastly blue, with a small square of reinforced glass.

It's not, I think. It can't be that. My stomach sours and I peer through the glass to a closet of sorts, a tiny painted concrete room with nothing but a single poster inside. On the poster's a slogan in large black letters: "Take slow, deep breaths and count to 10."

I pull back and point. "You put him in there?"

He shrugs with a look that says, *What can you do?* "It helps some of the kids calm down."

Does it? I'm shocked. "It's a prison cell." Only smaller, I think. Even if it works, is it really the right way to be handling kids?

He reaches up and scratches his neck.

So this is how schools 'manage' behavior like Konner's then. They penalize. Scare.

I honestly don't know what to say to the man. But the sooner I can get Konner out of this place, the better, I think. "Okay, well, thanks." I turn away, guiding Konner along with me.

There has to be a better solution than this.

Doesn't there?

Chapter 5

Belly of the Beast

A

few

weeks

later,

we've

hired a

different

psychiat

rist, a

tall

gentle

Konner, 6, at his first (and last) football game, 2008

bearded man, who's already started Konner on meds. It's

the same anti-convulsant drug that the first psychiatrist

recommended, normally used to treat epilepsy, and the

doctor says it's can balance out moods in kids like Konner.

Not that he's seen many like him before: kids who happen

to have autism as well as unpredictable shifts in mood.

"Meaning bipolar?" I asked him once. A word that

scares me. But also makes sense. He toggles so fast

between loud and uproarious laughter and mean and

aggressive fits.

The doctor holds up a pen. "Not necessarily." He

sits directly across from me, surrounded by stacks of

orderly mess. Papers and books are piled on tables against

the wall, sloped this way and that, like stacks of flattened

river rocks. "Some kids, and adults, have trouble regulating

their own moods." He wiggles the pen around in the air.

"Their brains do, that is. In Konner's case, I would call it a

mood disorder." He smooths out his hands, holding his pen

like a conductor's baton, guiding his point to a simple

close. "If we find the right medication that works, it can even things out."

"If?" I say.

"The key is finding what works for Konner and his illness, as well as his chemical makeup. It may not be the first drug we try."

I feel like I'm sinking into some wet and crumbly sand. "How long do you think?"

"To see if this works?"

I guess. "Yes." How long do we have to battle this thing? How long till he's free? Let alone me.

He holds the pen in both of his hands. "Let's give it six months."

That sinking sensation is getting faster. Six months, I think. Do we have six months? "It's a long time to see if it works."

He lowers the pen to his lap. "It is. Unfortunately, nothing works overnight."

*

Three months later, he's back in his old school again, holding himself together somehow. Though he's worse than ever with me at home. Screaming. Kicking. Pushing. Turning his room upside down. And draining me of all my energy.

Like today. A clear bright Sunday morning, and surprisingly warm for wintertime. We should be outside, hiking up to some beautiful lookout. Instead, I stand in the kitchen and stare at the ruined game board I'm holding up. And dreading the fact that Derrick's about to leave us again.

Derrick steps in and slides the screen door closed with a thwack. The smoky smell of natural wood chips floats in with him, the smell of the grill. But he stops abruptly. He knows my look. And he hears the screams. "What did he do?"

"This," I say. I hold up the board of a cheap chess set. It's bent and ripped at the cardboard corners. "I beat him at chess so he pinched me and screamed and tore this apart."

He's still screaming upstairs.

"In his room?" Derrick says.

"And throwing things." I'm furious, trembling. "I gave up my job. My life. For this. To deal with this kid. And he swung at me, almost hitting my face."

"Did you take him down to the floor?"

"Derrick." I tilt my head down, exasperated with him now, too. He wants to know if I physically overpowered Konner until he was calm. An exhausting feat for me these days. "He's bigger. It's hard. I'm not like you. I can't just overpower the kid."

He growls. "I'm worried. He's going to hurt you or Brennig one day."

"I'm worried, too." But at 6 years old and 100 pounds, muscular pounds, Konner's nearing my weight already. "If it happens again while you're gone, I'll have to." Like later, I think, when Derrick heads back to Detroit and something small and insignificant sets Konner off.

It makes me sick just to think about it. But I lift my head. The screaming has stopped. The thumping, too. We both look up.

So is Konner calm? Or is this the 'eye,' as the storm swirls and rages around us? I hear the thump of feet on the stairs and I tense for it.

A moment later, Konner's chocolatey eyes appear in the doorway. "What?" he says, like a teenager.

"Mom told me what." Derrick's deep voice is angry, clipped. "Why did you think you could leave your room?"

Konner shrugs. "I'm not angry now."

I could smack this kid, he makes me that mad.

Derrick steps toward him, hands on his waist, and looms over Konner. "You pinched your mom."

"Yeah? So?" Like I said. A teen. And he's only 6.

My anger dissolves and leaves me exhausted and jittery. "I can't do this," I say. To Derrick. Konner. I'm not really sure. I round the island where I stuff the game board into the trash. This constant battle for control with Konner, this taut and grueling tug-of-war, is pulling me down, under the toxic and muddy surface of whatever this is I'm thrashing in, and sooner or later I'm going to drown. "I need some air."

Derrick shoots me a worried look.

I sag beneath it.

"Go ahead," he says. "Do you want me to pick up Brennig, too?" Who's four now. He slept over at his cousin's house last night, doing all the fun little boy things he doesn't seem to get to do here.

"That's okay." I reach out and press a button. The garage door rattles up. "It's not quite time to pick him up." And I'm desperate to do whatever will keep me away from Konner.

I walk down our steep curved driveway, thinking it looks like a snake ready to strike my leg. Behind me I hear a piercing scream and I wince, go stiff. It's almost as if a bomb's gone off.

When I reach our narrow country road, I pause, conflicted, not knowing which way I should head in the short bit of time I have. I lift my gaze to the towering oaks and pines above. They make me feel small, as small as I do as a mom these days. My legs feel rubbery, loose, too loose to hold me up, and I buckle and sit on the grassy hill that borders one side of the driveway.

From the house comes another high-pitched cry, followed by a deep and angry shout. I close my eyes. What's wrong with this terrible child of ours? And what's wrong with me for wishing he hadn't been born to me?

I'm low and running on fumes. I am. How can I handle another sixty seconds of this, let alone a day while Derrick's away? I press the flat of my palms into my hot, moist eyes. And try to think of a positive here.

I deflate a bit as I let out a sigh. And then I finally think of one. *At least he's able to manage school.*

I rub my eyes and lower my hands. Yes. That's definitely a positive thing.

Tomorrow, I'll get a few hours to myself. To sit in front of an empty screen and type a tangle of meaningless words, while I worry and wait. For the phone to ring.

*

The next morning, my cell phone vibrates against my hip, inside my purse, where I sit in a carpeted waiting room waiting to have my blood drawn.

Instantly tense, I slide out my cell. Sure enough, the name of Konner's school glows on the screen. I peer around.

The waiting room is small and overly quiet. A handful of other patients sit, bored, and stare at their screens or magazines.

But I can't leave now. I'm all checked in. I breathe in slowly to steel myself, then let it back out. I press the phone to my ear. "Hello?" And I speak as softly as I can in here.

"Mrs. Johnson?" The principal's voice this time. I recognize it. "Konner's okay, but I'm afraid we've had an incident."

My hand shakes where it's holding the phone. "What did he do?"

Her voice is smooth and unreadable. "He punched his teacher." Punched. With a fist. "In her back, in front of the rest of the class. The kids are pretty upset right now."

Of course! They're six. What's wrong with my kid?

I can barely breathe. I can't take it in. I can't believe he did that in school. But what do I say? "Is she okay?"

"It aggravated some back issues she's dealing with."

I close my eyes.

Her accusation hangs in the silence between the words she's said and hasn't. My fault, I hear in her voice. My fault. I'm a terrible mom with a terrible child. "Where is he now?"

"Our school psychologist has him right now. I'm afraid she had to restrain him this time. When she went to try and calm him down, he swung his backpack and tried to hit her as well as some of the kids in class. I'm going to need you to pick him up."

Punched. Restrained. Swung. Hit. He's a monster, I think. And I just want to drive, drive until I reach the salty and billowing air of Ocean City, New Jersey, a few hours south of here.

I remember that morning I stretched in bed in the comfy old seaside rooming house. The window was open and it smelled of salt and bacon and sweets. Somebody was cooking breakfast somewhere. To my left, my sister, Laurel, slept curled in her bed.

Somebody knocked.

I rolled out of bed and padded to the door. It was early but I already knew who it is.

My dad. A quiet and gentle man. He loved to walk the boardwalk while all of us slept in the morning, and bring back gifts.

I opened the door. Dad, my daddy, smiled back at me, his hair still askew from walking outside and his glasses a little bit steamed with sweat.

He held up a bag and smiled at me.

"Thanks, Dad!" I could smell the cinnamon buns inside, their warm gooey smell.

If I could, I'd go back and hug him, too. It's too late for that now. The past is the past. It's also too late not to have kids. All I have is today. And honestly all I want is to flee, to drive down that place in Ocean City, rent a room and never come back again.

Instead I tell Konner's principal, "I'll be right there."

I walk to the nearby desk and say, "I'm sorry, I have an emergency."

I'm a slave to this child. And in two more months, when school lets out, I'll have him full-time. It's a fact I've dreaded for weeks on end. I can barely handle him the rest of the time.

I squeeze the wheel and drive to the school. And my stomach churns with a bitter dread. Derrick's away. I can't reach his cell. What would I say to him anyway? What good would it do while he's trying to work?

I shake my head through the blur of tears that threaten to fall. This is my weight to shoulder, alone. And I force my mind to stay strong for him. Stay strong for the boys.

I slide into a spot and park, and the day is filled with the sounds of children playing on the outside equipment nearby. Happy sounds. Shouts and screams.

Foreign sounds.

I press the buzzer on the brick wall and the front door clicks. I open the door. After a couple of breaths, I walk in, forcing myself to move at a tall confident pace, knowing the expressions I'll get. Cold, surreptitious looks. I walk through the main office door and give the glamourous heavyset woman behind the desk an exhausted smile.

She barely glances up at me. She clutches the phone in her ringed hand and speaks in a voice too soft to hear.

Then she sets the phone down with a click. "She'll be right out."

To my left, a door pushes out and the principal waits in the silly mismatching farm clothes she promised the kids she'd wear today. She holds out a hand. "Mrs. Johnson."

I shake it. It's limp. Which tells me a lot.

"I'm glad you're here. This way." She turns.

I follow her through the doorway into a room as square and stuffy as you'd expect in a school, with old worn pieces of furniture and lots of pictures of children hanging and propped on her desk.

Hidden behind her boyish frame and her brisk clipped walk, is a glimpse of Konner, standing beside a functional chair, and I'd like to shake him. Shake him so hard and scream at him.

When she steps aside to let me by, I see that his face is flushed and moist and his little pink lips are trembling. His eyes are glassy and he's fighting the tears that roll down his face.

"Oh, baby," I say. My heart can't take it. It melts for my son. My son who's been curled in the monster's belly. *This* is my son. He doesn't usually like to be touched, but I can't help myself. I drop to my knees and sweep my boy, my precious boy, into my arms. "I love you, baby. No matter what."

I feel his fluttering sobs against me. The press of his head. And the way he's sagging into me.

"We're going to figure this out, okay?" I feel the principal's gaze on me. I turn my head. "How long should I keep him home?" I say.

Her hands are clasped in front of her. "I'm afraid he can't come back, Mrs. Johnson."

109

I blink. I'm not sure I've heard her right.

"We can't handle his aggression here. It isn't safe for the other kids."

Or staff, no doubt. "I don't understand. Where will he go?"

"You'll need to write a letter to the Committee for Special Education to set that up. I'll mail you the information you need."

Special. Something is wrong with my son. I know that. More than anyone else. And the school is calling it *special*. Cute.

Does she see my child and his bloodshot eyes, and the terrible way he suffers inside? But, no, her eyes are only on me. Emotionless. Wanting another apology. Should I grovel now? I straighten up, holding onto Konner, keeping him tightly pressed to my side. "I appreciate what you've done for us." Whatever that is.

I lead my son away from her tense and watchful eyes and he slips his moist hand into mine. It's the first time in years he's let me hold his hand like this. And despite all the things I'm facing now, new school, new meds, more screaming, no doubt, I'm stronger somehow. I know what to do. I'll call the doctor, first and foremost, and tell him it's time to change the meds.

Then I'm going to kill this monster, this terrible dragon. I am. And free my son who's trapped inside. If it doesn't manage to kill me first.

Chapter 6

Scared to Sleep

Thunder growls in the distant hills, stalking me, as the bus pulls up. It's two years later, and our whole school situation has changed. And hasn't. Konner's having as many problems as he ever has.

Konner, 8, and Brennig, 6, in our backyard, 2010

"Hey, bud," I say in a too-bright voice. "I missed you today." If only I could say that and actually mean it. I want him to feel loved, though, no matter how awful his day has gone. So I put on the face I think he needs. The one that won't make things any worse than they are.

Konner steps off the bus onto the driveway. He's 8-years-old. And his face is flushed and his hair is slightly disheveled, too, though any third-grader could look like that. I have some inside info, though. I know how most of his day went. And it wasn't good.

The driver waves, partially hidden behind her sunglasses.

"Thanks!" I call as the doors close.

Thunder growls in the distance again and the bus chirps. She puts it in gear and rolls away. It's a 'little bus,' just half the size of a regular bus, a bus that's mocked by parents who know what it means. *Special.*

They're shuttling Konner to a different school in our district now, to see if the setup works for him. He splits his time between a smaller, quieter special-ed class and a louder busier mainstream room with twenty-some kids. He even gets extra support from an aide who's assigned to help him function in there. The experience has been, how should I say it? Bumpy so far.

I hold out a hand. "Can I take your pack?" It's a bit of a hike for tired legs. And I'm sure he's tired after what went on in school today.

Without responding, he dumps his pack on the pavement, without even meeting my gaze.

I stare at it, nauseated with worry now. "Hungry?"

He nods.

We trudge up the driveway in a bubble of silent tension. "Tough day?" I ask

He doesn't answer. A few splatters of rain smack the pavement, turning it black, as if something gruesome looms overhead, its mouth dripping acid and eagerness.

"Well, let it go." And I try to shake the feeling off. "We don't have to talk about it." That's my tactic today. Let it all go.

*

Two hours ago, his special-ed teacher texted me, a strong generous Puerto Rican woman named Mrs. Cortés who sees who Konner is underneath his monstrous moods. She said there'd been some trouble in class, and his mainstream teacher, Mr. Richter, would follow up with me.

More bad calls. It's why I hate hearing the phone ring.

When it finally did, I picked it up, my fingers tight, braced for the worst. "Hello?" I said.

115

"Mrs. Johnson?"

"Yes?" Why did we go through these trivial dances? These formalities? I was tired of them. He knew why he was calling. I knew why he was calling. I just wanted to get to the point.

But Mr. Richter was gentle with me, despite the fact that his voice was perplexed. "Mrs. Cortés is still with Konner," he said. "But I wanted you to know the details of what transpired today. Since I know you need to call the doctor and tell him."

"I do. Thank you." More calls to make.

Mr. Richter cleared his throat. "Well then, we were all working on a fun and simple project. Cutting out states and gluing them on a map as we work to memorize capitols. But Konner became agitated. He threw a glue stick and some other supplies onto the floor."

I could hear the nervousness in his voice.

"He had this really angry look," Mr. Richter said, "and was clenching his fists open and shut. Something I haven't witnessed before."

Something I have.

"The other kids backed away from him. So I asked him what was wrong and tried to diffuse the situation as best I could. He said he didn't like glue on his hands."

Because it's sticky, I thought. Sticky fingers make Konner upset. It had never occurred to me that something like that could be so upsetting, but it was starting to make some sense for me now.

"At that point," Konner's teacher said, "everything seemed to go wrong that could go wrong. All the other kids were looking at him and he started to scream. He told them to stop staring at him. He grabbed his chair and lunged at a boy. Luckily, Mrs. Cortés ran in and grabbed the chair. The aide called her the moment he flared.

I was glad to hear it. "What did she do to calm him down?"

"She told him to stop, that we don't hurt friends, but he started to shout that the other boy wasn't his friend. She lowered her voice and asked if he wanted to wash his hands in the teacher's bathroom down the hall. He said he did. He'd started to cry, and he let her lead him out of the class."

"I'm glad no one was hurt." I sighed. "I've definitely noticed some sensory issues. With foods and textures. Gel in his hair. Having to wear a football helmet. But he's never reacted this badly before. I'll tell his doctor. Thank you so much. The details help."

"Of course," he said, sounding hesitant now. "You should also know that Mrs. Cortés and I spoke at length.

We think it's best for Konner to stay in her class for now, until the doctor can sort things out."

Medication, I thought. That's what it always came down to now. My mentally unstable son needed meds. I felt myself droop. I thought the medication was helping. Maybe. A little, at least.

But I didn't now. Were medications even the answer here?

*

Back in the kitchen, I lean Konner's backpack against the table.

Konner trails in from the garage, moving so slowly it almost seems purposeful. Maybe he's worried I'm going to punish him for what happened in school.

I won't, though. I refuse to double up on consequences. It makes things worse. The school's already pulled him out of his mainstream room, and taken away his recess time, and I'm not going to pile anything else on top.

So I turn and say, "Would you like your afternoon treat before you do homework today?"

He trudges past, leaving the door to the garage wide open so a fly zips in. Little signs, I think. Little warning signs. Like dropping the pack on the driveway instead of handing it to me. Testing me. I stride to the door and close it with a swift, definitive whump.

Behind me, Konner mumbles something I can't make out.

"What was that?" I move to the fridge and pluck the ice cream container out, trying to remain cheerful, buoyant, hoping the mood will loosen him up. "I couldn't hear what you said, honey."

He sits at our round kitchen table with a dour face. "I don't have any."

"Any what?"

"Homework."

"I set the frosty container down on the countertop. "Mr. Richter told me you did."

"I don't."

Great. Like any seasoned parental soldier, I can sense the angry gusts of rain that are gathering. And I'm afraid of them. Not only that, but Brennig's about to arrive home, too. "Why don't I scoop your ice cream out, while you check your pack. Just to be sure."

He growls, deep down. An animal ready to spring at its prey. But he leans over and digs in his bag.

I scoop vanilla into his bowl. We've been gluten-free in the house for months, to see if it helps improve his moods, but it hasn't yet. I sprinkle allergen-friendly chocolate chips on top and wonder why I'm bothering. It should have helped him ages ago.

Konner lets out a piercing shriek. I startle and drop the spoon on the counter where it clatters loudly.

Konner stands hunched on the other side of the kitchen table, clutching a black composition book in both his hands.

I round the counter, one hand up, afraid to get too close to him. "What's wrong?" I say. But I already know.

His face is a bright and angry shade, and he starts to wail.

I rest my hand on the island, needing to hold onto something, and I raise my voice. "You have homework?" I say.

He howls at that, and I look at the clock. In three minutes, Brennig is going to walk into this mess.

"Honey," I say, and I pick up the bowl of ice cream, along with the spoon. "I have to look out for Brennig's bus." I move toward him, keeping the table between us. "Why don't you eat for now—" And I lean across and set down the bowl and spoon at his spot. "I'll help you look at the homework later."

He grabs the bowl with his hands and throws it, discus-like, sideways into the family room.

"Konner!" I say.

The bowl hits the ottoman and bounces off, splattering chunks everywhere, then drops onto the rug and rolls. Meanwhile, our frightened cat flies off the couch she'd just been sleeping on, two feet away from the spot where the bowl first struck its mark.

"That almost hit Mischief!"

I hear a knock on the door, followed by a bell ring. "Oh no!"

Somebody is twisting the metal knob.

I point at Konner, walking away. "Upstairs now! You need to calm down."

Through the oval glass of the front door, I see Brennig's cheek and eye pressed to the glass, looking in. Looking for me. To escape the menacing clouds outside.

"Sorry!" I call. I twist the bolt and open the door. Another low rumble of thunder greets me.

"Hi, Mama." He gives me a soft honeyed smile and steps inside.

"Sweetie, I'm sorry!" I wave at the driver who's paused at the bottom of our driveway to wait. "Thank you!" I yell, since, technically, she only has to wait for

124

Kindergartners to get inside. And Brennig started first grade this year.

She beeps twice, two happy beeps. And the brakes let out a rubbery squeal. The bus speeds off.

I close the door and practically run into Brennig's back. He's stopped dead in the entryway.

Konner stands hunched in the door to the kitchen, holding his arms away from his sides.

Brennig breaks to the left instead and darts upstairs.

"That's enough, Konner!" I say, feeling spooked.

He stands there, breathing, about to explode, and my mind races around in these looping figure eights, trying to grasp for (tactics, I think), a tactic I might have picked up from Konner's counselor, or that class on parenting strong-willed kids. *Anything.* But my mind's a blank and all

I hear is my heart rushing inside my head. I'm afraid, I think. Afraid of my son.

Lightning flickers at the edge of my vision. But the real threat's here, inside with me.

I stand stock still to see what he does. It's ridiculous. I'm the adult. I need to act. To *do* something. "I told you to go to your room," I say.

He doesn't react.

"Should I call your dad?"

His face twists with a monstrous rage and he screams so loud I can't hear anything else. Then he launches at me.

There's only one thing I can think to do.

I widen my legs and stiffen, braced, my heart thumping against my ribs, but he stops just short of tackling me.

His hand flies out and he pinches me, hard. On my forearm.

"Ow! Stop it right now!" But they're only words, just a bit of moist breath that floats above me and dissipates.

He pulls back his leg, about to kick, but I dodge to his right and grab him, pinning his arms to his chest. With a lot of muscle, I struggle him down to the glossy wood, where Brennig's backpack lies abandoned.

Konner struggles against me and screams.

"Calm down!" I say. "I'll let you go when you calm back down!" I'm holding him just in the right spot, so he can't lean over and bite my arm, and he can't free himself. All he can do is kick at the area rug nearby and grunt and scream.

I hold on tight, with a strength infused by adrenaline, a strength I only get when I wrestle him down to the ground like this. I think of those guards at the school with those awful quiet rooms. The guards who seemed to think strong-arming kids was funny. It's not. And Konner's growing, getting bigger every day. What happens when he gets too big for me to muscle him down? What is he going to do to me then?

Kill me, I think. And anyone else who makes him mad. And the ideas aren't funny at all.

He's heaving but isn't moving now.

"You calm?" I say.

He shakes his head. That's good, I think. At least he knows.

"Will you go upstairs if I let you go?"

He doesn't respond.

And I don't really know what to do with him. I open my arms, like springing a trap, and he scrambles upstairs on his hands and knees, wailing again. A moment later, his door slams shut and the glassware we keep in the dining room hutch tinkles softly against each other.

My arms have started trembling. Overhead, I hear muted thumps and shouts that come from his room. Later, I know, I'll find his mattress overturned, and his toys and clothes scattered around. Who do you think's going to clean that up?

I press my hands to my face and sob, but quietly, to the hard uncaring walls around me, to the house where I'm somehow in charge of a monster. Helpless. Alone.

I can't do this anymore. I can't.

A thunderous clap shakes the house and the lights flicker. I'm curled in bed with the lights still on, thankful we haven't lost power yet.

The home phone rings. A sound I hate. But this time Konner is home, in his room, passed out from screaming, and I've already fed Brennig and put him to bed.

I grab the cordless off my nightstand. The number calling is Derrick's cell. And I want to scream and rage and sob at the sight of it. Why does he get to escape this mess? Why do I have to carry it all?

Rain hammers the roof overhead, and I feel like hitting something myself. Unfortunately, I don't have the luxury of throwing some sort of adult tantrum. I still have two little kids in the house.

I press the button. "Hi," I say, through a knot that feels like a hand on my throat. I'm restless, completely twisted inside, and I walk downstairs, the phone to my ear.

A pause. "What happened?" He can read my voice.

I slip onto the front stoop, hoping the slap of the rain outside will drown my sobs as I fill him in.

His voice sounds farther away. More tense. "Did you call the doctor?" he asks.

I smash a tissue against my nose. "He wants us to see a specialist. Someone who knows how to handle difficult cases. Using a cocktail approach."

"Unbelievable."

Rain glimmers like silvery shards against the dark. "In the meantime, he's adding another med. Something Konner can take on demand. An anti-psychotic."

"How fast does it work?"

"Fast. In a few minutes or so. If he's willing to take it when he's upset." I pause. "It's not going to help him at school." I can hear the angry sounds as he breathes.

131

"Okay," he says. "Let me know when you schedule the specialist. I'll take the day off."

I swallow the bulging knot in my throat. I feel like such a terrible mom. Look at my child. And all these pills I'm stuffing inside him.

"I'm sorry, baby," Derrick says. "So sorry you have to deal with this."

I take a shuddering breath. "It's okay." But the last thing I feel is okay.

"I'm meeting up with some other guys for dinner soon. Can I call you later?"

I rub my nose. "It's okay. I'm tired. I'm going to bed." Still, I wish we could leave the line open and fall asleep, the way we used to do in college. But we say goodbye and I hang up the phone.

A rainy gust tugs at the house and the tears trickle freely again. They're icy this time, coming from some cold dark reservoir inside, a lake I'd prefer to drown in if it's able to stop this pain.

I walk back in and close the door as quietly as I can. It's raining so hard it feels like the rest of the world has washed away from the house and left me alone.

*

Minutes after I turn out the light, somebody screams.

I throw off the covers and stumble into the hallway. A flicker of lightning reveals two doors ahead of me. Konner's and Brennig's.

Another scream pierces the house. Different from Konner's. Panicky. Scared.

"Brennig!" I open his door, flip on the light, and sit on the bed with a leg folded under me. His eyes are open and looking through me. He's not awake.

I touch his arm. "Brennig, honey! Brennig, wake up!"

He splutters and coughs and I rub his chest to wake him up the rest of the way. After a moment, I press my hand to the side of his face. It's soft and hot. "Just a bad dream."

Thunder rumbles outside his window. He turns his head to look at me.

"It's okay, baby. It wasn't real."

He nods. "It was." And he lets out a hot liquidy cough.

"Oh baby." I gently rub his arm. "Can you tell me about it?"

His tears roll down, shiny in the glow of the overhead light. "A man," he said. "In the house with a knife."

My skin prickles with goosebumps. "Scary." No wonder he screamed. "But I promise there isn't a man in the house with a knife, okay? The alarm's on and we're safe inside." But I suddenly feel like something is here in the house with us and is watching us.

He peers at the door. "Can you look?" he says in his sweet high 6-year old voice.

I pat his chest. "Do you want to come?"

He shakes his head.

"Okay, I'll go look. Then I'll be right back." I still can't shake that feeling that something is watching me. Tense, alone, I peek into all of the downstairs rooms, flicking on lights one at a time, with the rain and thunder pursuing me.

Then I flip on the light to the hallway and stairs, feeling like something is right at my back, and hurry back up to the second floor. I check all the rooms and closets, too. Except, of course, for Konner's. Since Konner—

I stop, suddenly paralyzed.

A man with a knife. Those were Brennig's own words.

Konner's rage combined with his impulsive behavior has always scared me. For years I've worried Konner was going to stab me to death in my head while I slept. Something I've only told Derrick so far. And now Brennig's having those same fears, too. That dizzying feeling of déjà vu is too much for me.

I rub my arms and try to slow my breathing down, then I finally walk into Brennig's room. "All clear!" I say. "Think you can sleep?"

He shakes his head.

"Yeah, I'd have a tough time, too." I switch of the light, then I nudge his arm. "Scooch over, okay? I'll lie down with you till you fall asleep." I nestle against his back and throw my arm over him. "Better?" I say.

"Better." He sighs.

I can feel the thump of my heart, and his.

Soon, I hear his heavy breathing. He's asleep again. But I stay where I am and stare at the back of his pale head. Lightning flickers, confirming we're both alone in the room with a big queen bed. But I still feel a bitter tension inside.

"I'll never let anyone hurt you," I whisper. "Never. I promise."

A distant grumble of thunder responds. And that's
when I know.

I'm going to find it. Whatever it is that's going to
get Konner well in the end. If it's the last thing I do.

I'm going to call this special psychiatrist bright and
early and do whatever the heck he says.

*

"Happy birthday, baby." I lift my wide fluted glass,
ringed with blue. It's a margarita.

Derrick clinks his glass against mine. "To finally
getting out," he says. It's been months and months without
a break.

"And it's not even for a doctor's appointment."

He rubs the side of his smooth head. "Can't believe
we have to wait so long to see this guy." This special child
psychiatrist.

A full three months. But we've almost made it. Just a few more days.

"He'd better be good." I sip my drink. It's icy and sweet. I look around. It's a chic Mexican restaurant, only ten minutes from home, with blue-tiled walls and wooden beams and a waterfall that cascades down a huge piece of rectangular glass. Couples and families chatter and laugh and silverware seems to clink everywhere.

My cell phone buzzes against my hip, and I glance down. I see that it's home. "Uh oh."

"The boys?"

"Hopefully just a bedtime question." I press the phone to my ear. "Mom? Everything okay?" But then I hear it. The sound of Konner screaming in the house behind her.

"Kristal," she says. "I'm sorry, honey, but you'd better come home."

A scream warbles my speaker so loud that I have to hold it away from my ear. When I bring it back in, Konner hollers in a monstrous voice, "I'm going to kill you! I wish you were dead!"

My heart shudders to a stop. The words of an 8-year-old. Derrick is looking intently at me and I hold up a finger.

"Did you hear that?" she says in a hushed voice.

"I heard it. Do you know what started it?"

"Dad cut up his burger. In chunks."

I close my eyes. For the last few weeks, Konner's wanted to eat his burgers whole with a fork. I forgot to tell them. "Hang tight," I say. "We'll be right there."

When I lower the phone to look at Derrick, I realize the monster controls us now. He controls where we go and what we do. He controls every minute of every day.

We're powerless.

I hate this monstrous child of ours. And I hate the lives we're living with it.

*

That night, while Derrick watches TV, trying to wind down from the screaming that continued for an hour and a half after we got home, I lie in bed in the dark and leak. I leak tears so hot they scald my cheeks.

I'm trapped. A prisoner. I just want to be free.

I'm curled up tight, knees to my chest, listening to the crickets chirp outside, while I stare out the dark open window. The moon is full, like a large yellow eye leering at me. And that's when the terrible thoughts start to whisper and whorl. I could leave, I think. Stuff a bag with clothes and slip out in the dark. Escape from the place. And deal with the guilt for the rest of my life.

Or, better, perhaps, I could drink down a mountainous palmful of pills. God knows, we've got enough pills in the house. And the pain of having to carry this thing's too much for me. I yearn for escape with all that I am.

Am I really thinking these dark sick thoughts?

"Stop it, Kristal," I hiss to myself. "Stop it right now." Then I lift my hand and whack my face. A whack that sprays the tears from my eyes and sets a humming buzz in my teeth. I'm stronger than that.

And the rigid knot in my chest smooths out for a moment or two. Derrick works hard to support our family. *Too* hard, I think. And me? I work as a full-time mom. A mom, I think. Fixing this child falls straight to me. I have to be here, driving this through. Because life, until then, isn't

ever going to be livable. For any of us.

Chapter 7

Switching Things Up

The sound of voices and bouncing balls echoes around the large gym. I keep my eyes glued on Konner, worried, hoping he's going to behave himself. It's his first special-needs basketball game, the last in a long string of sports that haven't gone very well.

I glance at Derrick to see if he's just as worried as I am. We've let Konner try quite a few sports: t-ball, baseball and football, too, (where the tight helmet did it in for him), in addition to skiing as a family. And our last venture: special-needs baseball. A bad idea. And a worse outcome.

The basketballs come out and the kids start dribbling around the court, shoes squeaking, balls thudding, practicing their throws. For now, Konner is taking his turn, but I sense a touch of frustration in him,

Konner, 10, and Brennig, 8, at Konner's special-needs baseball game

in the rigid way he's holding the ball. And the source of Konner's frustration could be absolutely anything. Too noisy. Too many people around him. Or anything at all.

He throws the ball, misses the basket and scurries to pick it back up again. His frustrations in trying to learn a

145

sport usually land him in a screaming fit. Last year, however, he swung at a baseball and missed three times, then flung the bat away so hard that his coach had to leap out of the way.

So baseball is out. And anything else that requires him to hold a *weapon*, of sorts. Like golf. Tae Kwon Do. Skiing, as I've said. No, this time we're trying basketball.

He throws the ball and it hits the backboard and bounces off. I'm holding my thumb and rubbing it hard. Again, since Konner is on the autism spectrum, we're trying him out on the special-needs team, hoping it'll be less stressful for him. Less competitive, too. And I'm hoping others will understand his behavior a little better, tantrums and all.

The coaches assemble the first two teams and

Konner's playing on one of them. I peer around at the rest of the team. It's an eclectic group, but most of the other kids have intellectual or physical deficits, which frustrate Konner, since he seems intent on winning every game he ever plays.

Konner at his first and only special-needs basketball game, 2013

The only other child on the team who's on the autism spectrum is passive and sweet. He's the polar opposite of Konner, in fact, and not for the first time I wonder why I couldn't have gotten a child like that boy. An easier special-needs child, I think. Or, easy to me. Instead

147

of a child who exhausts me as well as mortifies me with his monstrous fits.

The sound of the buzzer fills my chest and Konner's team dribbles the ball up the court. There isn't a clock. The kids have it a little easier there. Which is great for Konner, who tends to feel pressured whenever he's timed.

Nobody scores, so we watch the kids weaving back and forth between the two nets. After quite a few minutes, I realize no one's passing the ball to Konner today. He waves his arms around in the air and yells at his teammates to pass to him. But nobody does.

Warning sign.

Are they tired of getting yelled at? I wonder. Or don't they realize they're doing it?

I can feel the gathering storm inside the basketball gym. Can't anyone else sense it coming? Isn't anyone else afraid of it, too.

The buzzer sounds and Konner falls to his knees, the color of a watermelon's flesh. Nobody scored, and that's okay with everyone else. But it's certainly not okay with Konner. He hates to lose, no matter how many times we've said winning isn't what's important. Having fun is. But Konner screams.

I know that scream.

Derrick immediately takes off running, headed for Konner who's across the court, while I hang back, at a loss as to what to do with myself.

The coach manages to get there first. He tries to touch Konner, to give him a few comforting words.

No, don't! I think. And I nearly reach up and cover my eyes. He's going to flip out. Don't touch him right now. But there's no way to tell anybody else that.

Konner screams at the coach. "Don't touch me! You're the worst coach ever! I hate you! We lost and it's all your fault! Get away!" In front of an entire gym full of adults and kids, he screams, and they've all turned their heads to stare at him.

Please, I think. Stop staring at him. I can feel their looks shift to me next, since they know I'm his mom, and whether or not it's true, I feel their stark and disapproving eyes as well.

The coach backs slowly away from Konner, just as Derrick reaches them. He whispers to Konner and yanks him up onto his feet. With an arm around him, he takes him out from under the watchful eyes around them.

I move to follow, like driftwood, I think. I'm anchorless now, knowing we didn't fit in with regular families at all, and now we don't fit in with the special-needs community. It makes me sad. And a little relieved. Maybe I can stop trying now.

But where do we fit? part of me asks.

Nowhere, I guess.

Maybe I can stop feeling like I need to explain myself and my son to others. Maybe it's time to be me, a mess, while I get Konner the help that he needs.

*

My dad steps out of the restaurant booth a week later and hugs me tight. He has this calm and quiet strength that reaches into me, right to my core. And his hug makes me yearn to be small, a child, and free of this weight I carry.

My mom scooches out from the booth to say hello

to me. "I'm glad you could get away for lunch." She smiles

brightly, her eyes worried behind her glasses. She kisses

my cheek softly, and smiles.

My own smile's weary and thin.

The three of us slide into the booth and glance at the

menu. It's our favorite place to meet right now, a mix of

cushy diner booths, with the lights down low, and a menu

stuffed with savory meals.

I set the menu aside. I already know what I'm

having. A warm salad with shellfish on top, and fat gooey

strips of cheese. Comfort food.

"So what did this new specialist say?" my dad asks.

Dr. Ruben. Derrick and I met him last night, after

he spent some time with Konner, and I'm still trying to take

things in. "He said, for kids like Konner, who have these

crippling mood disorders, there isn't a single medicine able to treat all the parts of the brain affected. We have to use a cocktail approach. Multiple meds for multiple symptoms."

My dad nods and clears his throat. "So lots of medication, huh?"

"Unfortunately." And I hate it, too. But it seems like the only option we have. "He's barely functioning in school right now. Just puts down his head and refuses to work. Or screams and gets aggressive whenever they push him too hard."

My cell phone flashes to life by my leg, on the booth beside me. I pick it up. "I honestly can't take one more thing." I glance at my parents. "It's Konner's school. I'll be right back." I hit the button and slide from the bench. "Hello?"

"Mrs. Johnson? Hi. It's Mrs. Maustelle. I'm calling to tell you Konner had a major outburst in gym."

I push through the door, and a damp gust of wind hits me outside. It's a small modified gym class, I think. And a small shy group of Asperger kids. So why isn't it working for him? "What happened?" I say.

"Konner's team lost at basketball, so he chucked the ball at the coach's head, then had a complete meltdown about it."

The sky is a blustery mix of blue amidst dark gray clouds. "Is the coach okay?" I lean back on the restaurant's outer wall to avoid the occasional spritz of rain.

"It missed him," she says. "Barely, though. So Konner's talking to the school psychologist. He's calmer now. But it's certainly a concern if he isn't able to control himself."

I wipe some mist away from my brow. But I feel like I'm covered in a stain that can't ever be washed off. "We're starting a new medication tonight. We'll see if it

154

helps." Of course, all medications take time to work. And the time we have is breakable, borrowed. "I'll warn you," I say, "it's a slow process." The new doctor plans to add a new medication to what Konner's taking, one at a time, then eventually start stripping others away.

And, yes, it's going to be a lot of meds. It is. I don't see any other choice right now.

She clears her throat, though it sounds a lot like a bored laugh. If she was a doctor, I'd fire her ass. "Well, thanks for letting me know," she says.

I escape the rain and head inside. When I slide into the booth to see my food sitting there, my stomach lets out a sour twist and I no longer have an appetite.

Because of the teacher. Because of the meds.

"Everything ok?" my mom says.

How do I even answer that? I close my eyes. I've agreed to let the doctor throw meds at my child until something sticks. And his teacher hates him. And I can't seem to write five words that make sense. I can't ever relax. And I don't know how long until everything's going to get better. I don't. So I say the only thing that's real and honest.

"Not really. No."

There has to be something else I can do.

*

It's nippy outside, but neither of us seem to notice right now. Konner and I step into the barn, with stalls on each side, and breathe in the strong and earthy scent. I glance at him. He's 11 now. But he doesn't seem bothered by the smell at all. His eyes are latched onto the horse. It's tethered loosely to either side of the corridor, blocking our path.

A slight young woman with a pierced nose, wearing an old sweatshirt and boots, is brushing the horse. "I'm Samantha. You're Konner?"

He nods, his eyes as wide as they get.

"Would you like to try?" She holds out the brush.

He takes it from her, and she gives him some tips on how the horse likes to be brushed. "This is Cody," she says. "She's a rescue horse. We saved her from an owner who neglected her hooves. She's safe to ride, it's been a few years, but she still gets startled by sudden sounds. If she puts back her ears, give her some space."

A special-needs horse, I think. Wow. And she's going to work with my special-needs son. What are the chances I'd schedule a lesson at a place like this without even realizing it?

The horse swings its head, breathing a frosty plume of air, and sniffs at Konner.

He's calm and polite. I can barely believe it. "Hey, girl," he says in a high sweet voice as he holds up his palm.

She gives it a few eager licks.

He laughs. "Yeah, I like you, too."

Amazingly, within minutes it seems, Samantha has gotten him up on the horse in a helmet and gloves, and she's leading him out of the barn to a large outdoor ring. It's muddy and wet. Snow's heaped near the fence in piles, the ash of some wintry eruption we can't quite rid ourselves of yet.

I watch her lead him around the ring and stop here and there. From across the ring, her voice echoes so I only hear snatches of what she's saying.

Like 'trust exercise.' She holds up her arms over her head, then drops them again.

He nods. He's listening. He lifts his arms over his head, sitting atop that massive horse. Trust, I think. It's the opposite of fear and anxiety. Two of the main things that seem to be setting Konner off.

And I feel a fluttery sob in my chest. I stand at the fence with my lips pressed to my steepled hands. But it's Konner who seems completely transformed. Relaxed and free. Like something has lifted. The monster is gone. For the moment at least.

Maybe it's that or the cold sinking in, but the hairs on my body all stiffen at once.

From across the ring, Konner turns his head and grins at me.

"There." I laugh, though it's almost a sob. "There's my son."

But the dream ends as soon as we get back into the car. As soon he realizes he still has homework to do today. And the screaming continues until he's back in his room again.

*

I'm asleep, exhausted, dead asleep, when the crying wakes me. I sit straight up, bleary-eyed, and look at the clock. It's 12:01 a.m. For some parents, the nighttime wakeups ended before their children turned one. For me, it's a long never-ending cycle, whether it's Konner calling for me, or Brennig, freaked out from another dream.

This time the cries are Brennig's again. I can hear the sobs, mixed in with the louder panicky wails.

With a sigh, worn out, I push the covers away from my legs and weave my way to Brennig's bedroom.

Inside, I snap on the wooden lamp next to his bed. "Hey," I say, though gently, trying to coax him awake. His eyes are squeezed shut and he's whipping his head side to side.

"Hey," I say. I lay my hand on his chest and give him a little shake.

His eyes pop open. Shocked. He presses his hands to his ears. And melts into these bubbling sobs.

"Shhh," I say, and I sit beside him and reach for his hand, hoping to gently tug it down and to talk to him.

He yanks it away, panicky now. "Make it stop," he says in a rough and desperate whisper.

"Is she screaming again?"

He nods, both hands pressed to his ears, elbows out.

The screaming woman is visiting Brennig almost every night, and our counselor thinks it's Konner's screaming that's manifesting in Brennig's dreams.

I take his hand and, silently, I whisper a prayer for the screaming to stop in his head. I whisper until his sobbing slows as well as the up-and-down hitch of his chest. I lean over and kiss his cheek. It's moist. "Better?" I say.

He nods and takes a shuddering breath. Then he slips his arms around my neck, and I lie down and snuggle up next to him.

"Think you can sleep, baby?" I say.

He nods again.

"Okay." I let out a breathy yawn. "I'll be right here." But the nightmares won't stop until Konner's screaming finally does, and I'm starting to lose hope of that happening.

"Mom?" says Brennig.

"Yes, baby?"

"Thank you," he says.

I smile and kiss his moist cheek again. "Love you, sweet." And my eyes, so heavy, slide shut and I sleep, entangled with my son, who's breathing gently beside me again.

Chapter 8

Startling Similarities

I sit back on our stuffed L-shape couch in the TV room with my laptop open, hands on the keys, feeling stiff, wound up. An old and rickety Mischief sleeps on the back

Konner and Brennig on their first day of school, 2012

of the couch, behind my head, as close to me as she's able

to get. Her black fur's still as silky soft as it ever was, but patches of white streak her fur here and there and her whiskers have all finally gone white.I'm trying to write. Again. But it's tough. I feel totally spent, emotionally and physically, too, so all I'm doing is forcing a tangle of words onto the heartless screen. It's a feeling I think of as *constipated*, just pushing one word after another onto the page with an energy I don't really have these days.

After a tortuous hour of this, I growl, so loud that it startles the cat. She hops onto a couch cushion, then onto the floor, moving as fast as she can at twelve.

"Sorry, Missy," I say, using my favorite nickname.

"Who am I kidding?" I say to myself. "Nothing good is going to come of this."

I open a browser to check the news. And the words Breaking News are smeared in red across the top of my screen. "School shooting," it says, and the school's not far.

It's just over an hour away in a small shell-shocked Connecticut town.

Horrified, I press my hand to my mouth and watch the latest coverage. Coverage of the kids and teachers shot down by some crazed lunatic loner kid. Coverage of the grieving families, and community. Only, the more I listen, and the more they flash pictures up on my laptop screen, I realize the shooter was angry. Autistic. Isolated. He sounds, in a way, a lot like Konner.

At least as far as *potential* goes. And I wonder: Is that going to be Konner one day?

*

Two days later, Konner's counseling visit is over. And Konner goes down to sit in a little waiting room down the hall, while I pause to speak to his counselor, Jean. I close the door, leaving us alone in the comfy office. Aside from her desk, sit two leather chairs and a little loveseat, along with shelves that contain some knickknacks she's

gotten as gifts, and some boardgames she plays with her

younger clients.

"Everything okay?" Jean says.

I shake my head. "It's that whole thing in Sandy

Hook."

She gives me a grim and knowing nod.

"That boy," I say. "Who did all that. He reminds me

of Konner." I look at her, hopeful, almost expecting her to

say, "No, they're not alike at all."

Instead, she says, "I thought of that, too."

I shoot her a look that's scared, desperate.

"Do you keep any guns in the house?" she says.

I sigh and go loose and trembly all over. It's a really

great question. But chilling, too. Derrick and I talked about

getting a gun, just for protection, but we never actually

went through with it. "Thank God. No. That's something, I guess."

She nods, looking relieved, too. "But I'd tell the doctor. And get his take. It may be time to change his meds."

And we do.

We add an anti-depressant to what he's taking. But, like everything else, it can take a month or two to kick in. Or longer, since the doctor increases so slowly and carefully, to watch for potential side effects, including a worsening of Konner's condition.

But it weighs on me: the shooter's expression, which I've seen on the news. Detached, almost stunned. An expression I've seen on Konner's face, too. Yet the autism community is trying to distance itself.

I sit on the L-shaped couch again, my laptop closed on the cushion beside me, and I watch the news on the TV this time. The coverage is dark and so hard to watch, but I saw a promo for a segment I really wanted to see.

It flashes on.

It's an interview with the owner of a shop in town who came into contact with the shooter before the whole sickening thing went down.

The man is lanky and trembling, upset. Who wouldn't be? But he says something that pierces me all the way through my heart and makes me bleed. He wishes he'd killed the boy years ago, so the whole tragedy had never happened.

I sit there, stunned.

I can understand, I guess, in a way, the anger, the tears, after seeing what happened to all those precious kids and adults, but I can't understand wishing him dead.

Is that how little we understand kids on the autism spectrum? Especially kids who are filled with rage?

And the answer is, yes. People would rather see kids like that disappear or die to protect themselves, than face the challenge of helping them. Kids like my son. And by that I mean helping them *before* things like that ever happen. We'd rather call them 'mental' instead of admit they have a real and treatable disease that's based in the brain somewhere. A biological disease that still needs research and trial and error in order to treat.

All I know is this: I have to make sure my child doesn't turn into that. The question is how? And will I actually be able to do it?

I stand in the bedroom, too shocked to smile or even react. "You're sure it's free?"

Derrick hands me the printed email invitation. His company is sending us to Naples, Florida, for a long weekend. Just Derrick and me.

"A reward trip," he says. "For the work I put in out in Detroit."

"Airfare?"

"You name it. Food, activities, hotel. At the Ritz."

"Get out!" I laugh. I hadn't scanned down the page that far.

"And the boys?" I can't say it. My stomach gives a sickening lurch. My mind goes straight to the negatives.

"I'll ask my parents. I'm sure they won't mind."

I can feel the worry that tugs at my face. I'm not so sure. I think about the last time they came to visit. When

Konner threw a fit so big in his room that we all had to escape outside. Who'd ever want to be stuck with that? "What about Konner?"

"It's a weekend, babe. What do you think?"

"If something happens?"

"It won't. And if it does, my parents will figure it out."

I ignore the big clenched fist in my gut. I can't let my life be ruled by fear. Or Konner, I think. "Okay," I say. "If they say yes." But I don't really expect them to.

*

A month later, we lie on chairs on the sugary sand and I gaze at a sea so calm and clear it looks like a bathtub.

"I never knew the Gulf was so beautiful," I say. Or that I'd ever be able to breathe freely like this, without some guilty strap cinched tight around my stomach. "Let's move here. Okay?" And my skin is hot and moist with sweat, a feeling that makes me loose, relaxed.

Derrick says, "mmm," next to me, with his eyes closed, sunglasses on.

I'd forgotten how good it felt to unwind. At home, Konner was usually so bad my parents couldn't handle him. But then, two years ago, my parents moved to the suburbs of Phoenix to escape the snow and the high cost of living in New York State. The fact that Derrick's parents were willing to drive two hours south to handle a monstrous child, well, it meant more than a lot to me.

Still, I keep my cell phone in easy reach.

Almost as if it hears my thoughts, my cell phone flashes to life on the small glass table beside me. I catch a glimpse in the corner of my eye. My heart hiccups. I pick it up. It's our home number, but just as I'm about to say hello, it stops and the phone app disappears. "Your mom just called."

"She what?" Derrick lifts his head from the cloth-backed chair.

"You heard me."

"Why? Did she leave a message?"

I touch the voicemail app with my thumb. "Not yet," I say. I watch it for another twenty seconds straight without looking away. I shake my head. "Should I call her back?"

"Here." He holds out his hand. "If she needs us, she'll leave us a message. Agreed?" He takes my cell. "She said to relax. The kids are fine."

"Come on, Derrick." I hold out my palm.

"Don't worry. I've got it." He puts it on the table beside him. "For once you don't have to be on-call."

174

You'd think I'd be grateful to hear those words. Instead, I try to sit back and relax, but the sour squeeze in my stomach remains. I've been on-call both night and day for eleven years. I don't know how to let go of that. Or *if* I can. As much as I want to.

A few hours later, we sit in a cozy Italian place in downtown Naples. Dim. Tablecloths. The whole shebang. We enjoy our slippery homemade pasta with a deep woody glass of Cabernet, but before we finish, my cell phone hums to life in my purse, on vibrate mode. I lift it out. It's our home number. I show him the screen. "Guess you shouldn't have given it back."

"Or left it back at the hotel instead." Derrick's face looks clouded, tense. He needs this break as much as I do. "Here, I can take it."

"No, it's okay." I slip outside into the dark, where Derrick can watch through the plate glass window. The air's still warm, but cooler, divine, when I answer. "Joan?"

A sniffle answers. "Mom?" The voice is desperate.

"Konner?"

"Come home. Right now." He lets out a sniffling sob. "Please. I need you at home. Grandpa's mean. And Oma won't give me a treat while I'm doing my homework. She makes me wait until afterward."

All the relaxation I'd gathered so far, like the soft, wet sand I'd scooped over my sun-warmed skin, crumbled away. "Konner, we can't just leave, honey. Our flight isn't until tomorrow night."

His voice winds into a deeper sob. And while I feel for him, I can't help feeling manipulated.

"Why don't you let me talk to Oma? I'll make sure she—"

"No!" The line goes dead.

I hold my cell away from my ear and look at it. "Lovely." He hung up on me.

I lower my head and glance inside and Derrick raises his eyebrows. *Well?*

I shake my head. Then I tap our number in. It rings.

"Hello?" says Joan, my mother-in-law, her voice unusually reticent, tense.

"Hey," I say. "Konner just called."

She's quiet a moment. "I'm sorry," she says. "I tried to calm him down, but he stormed away with the phone. He's not feeling his best today."

"What happened?"

"Oh, please. Don't worry. I'll go in and talk to him. You guys need a break. Let us handle this."

It felt like a hand was kneading my stomach, and the rich and heavy meal I ate. "I'm worried," I say. "I know he's a lot to handle. I do. I'm sorry I left you to deal with him."

"Don't be. We're fine. And every small thing that makes him upset is just that, it's small. He doesn't want to do his homework. So he has a big meltdown and screams. He doesn't want to eat his dinner. So he has a big meltdown and screams. He's rude to Allan so Allan tells him to go to his room, so Konner tears the whole room apart. Sound familiar?"

"Yeah."

"Now listen," she says. "You handle things all by yourself when you're home. Old fogies or not, the least we can do is handle things here for another day." She laughs

out loud. "Don't worry. Have fun."

I look around at the warm brick-lined walk, and the

people strolling past and chattering without a care in the

world. People who don't have monsters for sons. And it's

no use. The sour twist in my stomach remains. It lives with

me. And now that I've tasted some peace and calm? I can't

bear it. I really can't bear anymore.

Chapter 9

Second Guessing

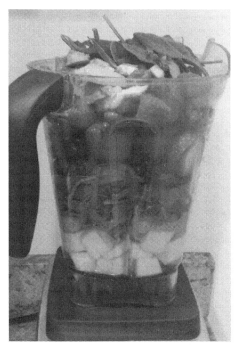

One of the many green drinks I made for the boys

"Lithium now?" Derrick leans back at his desk, arms crossed. The edge in his voice mirrors the knot I feel in my gut.

I stand in his office above the garage, hands on my waist to hold me up, tired from all the driving I've done, tired of carrying the weight of the specialist's recommendation, when nothing, nothing, seems to be working.

"I know," I say. "I like it as much as Must Tell's calls." Maustelle's, I mean. Konner's sixth-grade teacher. I've nicknamed her for her bad reports, since that's pretty much all I ever get. Despite the fact he has pretty good grades.

There's a knock on the door and a scrape as it opens, revealing the master bedroom beyond. "Mom?" Brennig peeks in. "What's for dinner?"

My shoulders sag. Konner and I just got back from a five-hour round-trip visit to Dr. Ruben, the pricey new child psychiatrist. And I'm tired, did I happen to mention that? "How about a toasted PB&J?"

"Yum."

"Okay. Just give me a sec."

The door scrapes shut.

I turn to Derrick. "We need to do *something*. He's awful at school. He screams in gym, and he throws things, too. And in class, he puts down his head all the time, refusing to work."

Derrick leans his smooth shaved head on the chair and glares up at the recessed lights. It's his I-can't-take-this-kid-and-his-drama anymore look.

"I know." I show him my hands. "I know."

Slowly, he rolls his head back and forth. He doesn't want to make the call either.

"How about this?" I round his desk and drop to the rug beside his chair and sit on my feet. "I'm reading a lot about gut health, you know, and all the processed chemicals we eat today. Some people claim they've been able to heal themselves and their kids of various illnesses."

"Kids like Konner?" His eyes roll toward mine, narrowed.

"Or similar, yes. All I can do is try and see if it changes anything. It's not that different from gluten-free. Except we can't eat out anymore. Or processed foods."

"Think about this." He lifts his head. "You're going to cook breakfast, lunch and dinner."

I shrug. "Do you have a better idea?"

"Snacks, desserts. All that stuff. You know how he is." Picky doesn't come close to it.

I wave a hand, thinking out loud. "I'll find simple recipes. And I'll try to remake what Konner likes in a healthier way." Granola bars. Donuts. Cookies. Carbs. "It's a good thing he likes apples, at least."

"And watermelon." He stares into space, shaking his head. "Okay." He shrugs. "If you think you can do it."

I imagine our boy off meds and *well*, and able to learn in a mainstream class. A regular kid with regular friends. For the first time in a long and horrible time I allow myself to imagine that. I can do it, I think. "We'll start tomorrow. After I hit the grocery store."

"And Kristal." His office chair squeaks. "If it gets too much—"

I lift a hand. "I know. I'll stop."

Famous last words.

*

I'm moving around the kitchen island, measuring out all the ingredients for the cookies the boys will eat after school. They're allergen-free chocolate chip cookies and high in protein. No carbs and no processed sugars either. No gluten, no dairy, no soy. No preservatives. They're also really shockingly good, with a soft chewy crunch you'll never find in a store-bought cookie.

Already that morning, I'd made high-protein chocolate donuts using a powdery almond-meal base. Then I'd sent Konner to school with his favorites: cashews along with a perfectly unblemished McIntosh apple, a savory-sweet granola bar made with salted sunflower butter, and the last two paleo oreo cookies I'd made from scratch. More sugar than I'd like, but overall not bad for a kid who could live on soda and chips.

If I stop moving, I might not be able to restart myself, so I push the thought out of my head. I knead the gluten-free chocolate chips into the sweet-smelling dough I've made, ignoring the fact that my writing is out of the question now. Healing Konner through cooking is all I can think about.

If I knew how to cook simply, perhaps, that would streamline things. And if Konner were willing to try to eat regular foods (a strawberry? a bite of cheese? come on) without a knockdown drag out fight, that would certainly help a lot, too.

The doorbell rings. My hands are greasy and slick with batter, so I rub them off onto a towel and walk to the door. Despite the autumn chill outside, the entryway's warm with the sun streaming in.

My sister, Laurel, is standing outside looking glamorous, poised, in a feminine jacket with fluttery sleeves, modeling the sparkly jewelry she makes. Behind her, under a cool blue sky, red and gold leaves cling to the scaly arms of the trees as if ready to flap and fly away.

Delighted, I open the door. "Hi!" A chilly gust makes me narrow my eyes. "Come in! Were you just in the area?" I hug her one-handed, holding the towel, feeling a

186

bit like a frump beside her. I'm showered and I have some makeup on, but I haven't bothered to blow out my hair. It's twisted into a knot at my neck, still damp from the shower.

She steps into the entryway and closes the door. "Sorry! I tried to call you first."

"You did?" I frown. Have I missed other calls? "I must have been in the shower. Sorry."

She holds up a soft silvery pouch.

"It's done?!" I gesture for her to follow me. "Just let me wash my hands off first." The company Derrick works for is having a Christmas party in three more weeks, and Laurel offered to deck out my dress with silver and gems.

I scrub my hands under the water, then wipe them off.

Laurel sits gracefully on the couch, smiling softly, her ankles crossed, with the pouch on the cushion next to her.

I scoop it up. "Yay!" Its heavier than I expect it to be. I sink down, happy to sit for a moment, and tug at the shimmery ribbons that hold it. But my thoughts go back to the phone. And Konner. And the school. Have they tried to call?

Two plastic sleeves slide into my palm. "Earrings, too?"

She flashes a wry and guilty smile. "They'll go great with your dress."

"Oh, Laurel," I say. I open up the necklace and lift it out. At the end of three long silvery strands hangs a trio of hammered metal circles. A shimmery stone, the color of champagne, hangs from the inner top of the circles.

"Like it?" She bites her lip, excited.

"It's stunning!" I hug her again.

She laughs.

I slide out the earrings next. The matching hammered circles tinkle against each other. But Laurel's wearing a funny expression. "What's wrong?" I say.

After a few heartbeats she says, "I'm worried about you and all this cooking, on top of the way Konner is acting. Are you really okay?"

My busy façade ripples and sags, and I set the jewelry aside on the couch. "I'm tired," I say. "Konner's teacher's calling me every day, telling me about every awful thing he does in school. And, of course, I need to know about them. But I know she doesn't like him at all. He's not like the other kids in her class. They're quiet and docile."

189

Laurel nods. "Obedient."

"Yes." I rub my hands on top of my jeans. "He's angry and mean. Believe me, I know. And nothing I do makes any difference."

"I'm sorry." She frowns. "I can only imagine what you're dealing with. But I wonder if you need to consider giving him that new medication, instead of taking this all on yourself."

I look at my hands. "But what if it works?" The cooking, I mean.

"And what if it kills you first?" she says. "How long can you really keep up with this?"

I feel a stiffening in my chest. I have to do this. If not me, who? "I know. You're right. I'll think about it."

But I don't, to be honest. I really don't. Because somehow, I'm sure, Konner's issues are all my fault. And so are all three of the meds he's on.

*

My eyes are closed, but I'm not relaxed. I'm starting to sweat. I'm up to my neck in scalding water in our master tub, hoping it melts my screaming muscles into submission. Two days ago, I ran my first half-marathon with a friend of mine, but, boy, my body is hating me now.

And I can't help but think about Konner, too, how his outbursts at school are pushing the other kids away, even the other Asperger kids. Some just retreat and hide from him. But regular kids respond differently. In the two mainstream classes he attends (with an aide, of course), some of the boys have picked up on Konner's primary weakness: the fact he gets so easily angered. And some of them have started provoking him.

Out in the bedroom, the phone belts out its awful song. Oh no, I think.

I glance at the floor, where I usually keep my cell and the house phone side by side whenever I come in here to shower. I'm always tethered to a phone these days. But no, for the first time ever, it seems, I've left both phones in the bedroom beyond.

The phone urgently trills again.

It's the school. I know it.

I spring to my feet and nearly slip, splashing water from the tub as I do. My towel sits on the rim of the big triangular tub. I dry myself most of the way, wrap the towel around me and hurry out into the bedroom. The boys are at school so Derrick's office, accessible only from our master bedroom, is open for now. And, for once, he isn't on a conference call.

"Sorry, babe," he calls to me. He keeps a muted phone on his desk. "I was finishing up on a call, so I couldn't take it for you."

"That's okay. I got it." I listen to the message. Sure enough, it's the school. The assistant vice principal to be exact. Mrs. Jarviss. And all she says is to call her back. "Great."

Clutching the damp towel around me, I dial the number and ask for her. Then I sit, perched, on the edge of the bed.

A moment later, the line hums to life. "Mrs. Johnson?" The female voice is cool. Reserved.

"Yes, so sorry I missed your call." My mom-guilt pinches me, sharp and hard. I should have carried the phones into the bathroom with me. So stupid, I think.

She speaks so slowly I can tell she's feeling out every word. "Yes, well, I have Konner here in my office now. He isn't hurt. Don't worry. He's fine. But he had some trouble with another boy in his mainstream class. He shoved the boy and he's still not able to settle down." There's a humming sound and the line gets loud. "I've put you on speaker so Konner can hear you."

I'm too surprised to say anything. She's going to talk in front of my son while I sit here on speaker?

"Konner," she says. "Your mom's on the phone. Would you like to explain what happened today?"

I hear him grunt and somebody murmurs.

"No!" he screams.

There's a scuffling sound, then other voices are murmuring now. How many people are in that room?

"Hello?" I say.

He starts to cry.

I stand. "Take me off speaker right now!"

There's a plasticky clattering sound in my ear, then Mrs. Jarviss speaks in a voice that's measured and cool. "Konner was hitting his head on the wall in my office just now. Could you please come down?"

I shake my head in disbelief. "How many adults are in that room?"

A pause. "Four."

"Four!" I say.

"One is our school resource officer."

"A cop?" I say, trembling, enraged. Instead of trying to calm him down, they intimidate him. And I think of those guards at the day treatment facility who bragged about taking a student down. Why do these schools use such hard-core disciplinary tactics first, when other methods—kinder, simpler, more thoughtful methods—can work so much better without humiliating the student, too, and making things worse? "You're freaking him out!" I tell the woman. "He needs to calm down before he can talk. And he isn't able to do that himself. He needs a quiet space and a person he trusts. Understand? Where's the school psychologist?" She's someone who's calmed him down in the past.

Another pause. A murmuring voice in the background. Great. A bunch of buffoons. "I believe she's with a student." *Believe*. So she isn't sure.

"Find her," I say. "My son needs her. And get those people out of the room!" And please, I think. Please, please, please. Don't escalate things any more than you have.

"Certainly, we'll try to reach her," she says. "And you're heading here now?"

I can hear it then. The strain in her voice. She's afraid of him. And she doesn't have a clue what to do about him.

To be fair, though, neither did I until I realized how they were handling him. "I'll be right there." And I tug on my clothes as fast as I can. Then I hang up and dial his counselor, punching the button that lets her know it's an emergency.

"Kristal?" she says.

"Konner's in crisis. Can you see him today?"

*

Ten minutes later, a woman from the office escorts me back to a conference room. The principal stands from the table to greet me. He's tall and stiff and his face is completely unreadable, and yet soft somehow. A permeable stone.

He shakes my hand and sits at the opposite end of the table. Mrs. Maustelle's there as well, on the other side, cheerful for once, so we sit in sort of a triangle, keeping our distance from one another.

"I understand your position," he says. "It's a tough one, I know. You're worried about your son and you're working hard to do what you think is best for him."

Soften her up, I think, before you lower the ax. "Thank you," I say, my hands resting on top of my purse.

He presses his hand to the front of his crisp blue business shirt. "I'm worried about my students, too. I worry about what's best for them. Their safety, of course."

My son is a danger. I can hear the words behind the words, words that are phrased so carefully.

"I wish it had worked out differently. But I need you to know, if Konner comes back to school in the fall and has another incident, he's going to be expelled this time."

It's the same script all the schools use. And I wait for it since I know he's not done.

"For good this time."

The thumpety-crack of the axe hits bone. And slices through to my beating heart. What the principal means is we'd better start looking for another school. A special-ed school.

Strangely, I feel the weight fall away. The weight of doing it all myself. And the weight of having to mainstream him. We'll look for a special-ed school without any quiet rooms.

If that school even exists out there.

Twenty minutes later, I glance at Konner in the rearview mirror, where he sits slumped in his seat behind me. His hair has warmed in recent months to an auburn color instead of blond, and his face looks angled, less baby like. "I'm sorry you had to go through that today."

His head is turned and he's facing the window, staring out at the rain-splashed street, at the houses crouching on either side that stare at us with their square dead eyes, as we head to see his counselor. "I wish I were dead," Konner says.

My gut suddenly feels like cement. "Oh, baby," I say. "I love you so much. It's hard to see you hurting like this?"

He doesn't respond. And I'm not really sure if he's listening.

"Okay, just know that the doctor sent a prescription in. You're going to feel better soon. I promise. And Konner?"

No answer. He continues to stare at the houses outside

"I won't stop fighting until you do. Do you hear me?"

A pause. And then, "Okay."

It's something, at least.

I move into the left-hand lane and slow as we near the turn ahead. There's nowhere to go but left, across three busy lanes. If only life was as easy as this when it came to making decisions, I think. Turn left, that's it. And you'll get to the place where you need to go.

Too often I feel overwhelmed by the ways I could slay the dragon and free my son. Cooking. Doctors. Social skills training. A typed routine, and constantly preparing him for what comes next. Special-ed sports. A rewards system. Consequences. The negative kind. Structured playdates (when the kids still wanted to play with him). Horseback riding. Medications, of course. When so few things actually seem to work.

For once, like the left I'm about to take, I know there's only one way to go. New meds, new school. That's it. No more. And somehow it's a relief not to have to think about everything else on top. Laurel was right. Derrick was right. But I had to figure it out on my own.

Traffic thins on the far-left side due to a red light farther down.

But before I take my foot off the brake, Konner says. "Mom?"

"Yes, baby?"

"Can you kill it?" he says.

The words startle me out of my thoughts. "What do you mean? Do you see a bug?"

"The anger I'm always feeling inside. It's makes me wish I were dead instead. I want it to stop."

The cement in my gut oozes into my throat now. I try to swallow it down but can't. Did he just say what I think he said? Did he tell me what he's feeling inside? For once, I'm stopped and there's nobody idling behind me, waiting, pressuring me into making my turn.

I keep my foot jammed on the brake and turn around as far as I can.

His head rests on the back of the seat, but he moves his eyes to look at me.

"Yes." And I give him a tough look. "Do you trust me?"

He nods.

"We're going to kill that monster with meds. The doctor already told me his plan. He knows what he's doing and I'm going to let him do it, okay?" I reach back and rest my hand on his thigh. "This is not your fault. Do you hear me?"

He nods.

"It's the monster that makes you angry like that. We'll kill the monster together, okay?"

A car slides into view behind him, and he puts his hand on top of mine. It's hot and puffy. I hold it tight as I turn away. And I drive one-handed across three lanes of empty road. As strong as I've felt in a long, long time.

*

Six weeks later, we're in the car scouting new schools.

My dreams of having a mainstreamed kid with a mainstreamed life are over. Gone. I'm okay with that now. My child isn't like other kids. He's special. So what? He has an illness, for heaven's sake, a crippling illness, and a heady mix of medication is the only real thing that makes a difference. That and riding around on a horse. I see that now.

Would a parent with a child who has asthma say, no, you're not allowed to have your inhaler today? You need to learn to breathe on your own?

The doctor's the one who told me that little analogy and it helps me a lot. It helps me let go of a lot of things. Of the concept I'm a bad mom, for one. And that I'm choosing to drug a behavior problem. Both notions are wrong. My child's disease just happens to impact various parts of his brain, versus one, so there isn't a single medication that treats every one of those parts. I wish there were, but there isn't. There's not.

However, there *are* some great medications that work. I know that now, too.

I rip open the white paper bag and twist the lid off the new bottle. "Here, baby." I turn in the car to hand him two pills, the ones that double his Lithium dosage to 1200 now. They're pretty capsules, bubblegum pink, belying the 'salt' that lies within, a salt that works even though doctors don't fully know why.

You know what? I'm actually okay with that. As long as it works. Because Derrick and I agreed that quality of life *today* is more important than some dreamy unknown tomorrow. It's time for us to start living *today*.

From behind the wheel, Derrick snakes his way along the narrow and curving highway. It's one of the prettiest drives in our state, but one of the most stressful to drive. It's a relief to let Derrick drive for a change. It's a relief he's able to come with us.

"Hey," I say, looking around.

Konner's gripping his cell phone tight on top of his lap. He's staring out at the oaks and pines that press in against the sides of the road, making it feel like we're in one of those torture presses. His brother stayed back with his cousins today, giving them each the space they need, so there's that at least.

"Nervous, bud?"

He looks at me and I see the tension that's burrowed into his chocolatey eyes. "What if they have a quiet room."

I could strangle whoever designed that concept for a child's school. A tiny prison with a lock that's fixed on the outside. Someplace a child can sit in and scream (and bang his head bloody) until he calms down.

I lower my chin so he sees my eyes, so he sees just how serious I am. "If they have one, we leave."

"Really?"

Derrick says, loudly, "Yes."

Konner peers at his dad. "Leave right away?"

I glance at Derrick with a grim smile. We've talked about this. "Like, tell the guy thanks but no thanks and leave."

Konner sits back. "Okay," he says with a little sigh. But he doesn't look fully relaxed either.

Derrick gives me a quick look. "So Ruby told you about this place?"

I smack his arm and laugh. "Ruben." All I need is for Konner to call the man *Ruby* next time we go. Though it is a gem of a nickname, I think.

I see the sign for our turn ahead, and hear the click of our turn signal.

Derrick guides the truck off the highway and follows the GPS through several turns, through a sprawling Westchester neighborhood where the tiny capes and ranches with lawns the size of a green mini golf strip are beautifully kept, but close together. It's amazing how much space you lose in order to halve your train ride into the city.

Smack in the middle of a neighborhood, Derrick slows and pulls into a complex of small brick buildings and parks. The school itself is out for the summer, following a slightly different schedule than our own district does, so we have the benefit of seeing it in more of a muted setting than last week's tour (quiet rooms and all). It gives Konner a chance to see what they offer without feeling overwhelmed, too.

"Which building?" says Derrick.

I point. To our left, a tiny brick building stands in the middle of the small campus, just on the edge of a parking lot and a small sports field with country grass. It's a little rustic, but that's okay. It's the inside I'm more concerned about, and the teachers, of course.

Derrick kills the engine. It's hot outside and the engine starts to tick like a clock. But none of us move to open our doors.

At the front of the building, a door pushes out. A man, young, but powerfully built, waves to us.

Finally, I sigh and push out my door, and Konner comes around to stand with me. I peer at his face but it's hard to read. He stares at the man, his body tense.

"Coming?" Derrick locks the car.

I hold up a finger. "One second," I say. Then I lower my head close to Konner's. "I mean it." I whisper. "No quiet room. We see it, we leave."

He nods, but his eyes don't leave the man.

"Together then?" I move and he finally follows me.

When we near the door, I see the man's eyes are a pale ice blue and tattoos loop out from under the sleeves of his polo shirt. Despite his tough outer persona, he beams with warmth. I don't know why, but I like him. I do. I can tell he's not one of those stiff-necked suits with a slow and carefully measured voice.

"Hi, Konner," he says. "I'm Mr. B." He places a palm on his big chest. "Unless you want to call me Mr. Baditella. Or Bad for short. You can do that, too."

Konner shrugs. His eyes roam around, but he's listening.

"I don't suppose you like chess, do you?" Mr. B says.

Konner's eyes widen. "You know how to play?"

I glance at Derrick, who looks impressed, then back at Mr. B again. "Konner loves chess. He plays competitive chess online."

Mr. B grins. "I could use a partner. My last one left for high school just a few weeks ago. Come on." He tosses his head behind him. "I'll show you around."

We trail after him, and listen to him talk about a normal day, the change of classes, and we peer into each of the rooms. A primary classroom, a small gym, a carpentry shop (complete with the smell of fresh sawed wood), a large science lab that also doubles as the art room, a kitchen, even a carpeted game room where kids can earn some time playing video games.

It's kind of stuck in the 80s, I guess, but it's homey, too. With the fresh plasticky smell of paint.

"How many kids in all?" I say.

Mr. B stops in the wide hall that runs the length of the little building. He leans against an open doorway and crosses his arms. "By law, we can only take eight each year. And we'll always have a teacher and an aide."

I'm not really sure I've heard him right. "Eight...to a class?

"Well, yes. Eight in the program, I mean. Eight in the school."

Derrick and I exchange a look. Amazed. To call it a *small private* school doesn't quite express it enough.

"One other thing." I step to the side to look in the class. It contains, amazingly, eight student desks, along with two larger teacher desks. There aren't any other doors to be seen. "Is there—?" I'm almost afraid to say it. "A quiet room?"

He thumbs at the room behind him. "In here." Then he steps aside.

My stomach cinches into a ball. Oh no, I think.

I feel the press of Derrick's hand in the small of my back. I peer inside. It's a conference room, with a big wooden table and soft leathery desk chairs.

"Kids can go there if they need some space" Mr. B says.

Their quiet room is actually a *conference room.*

I feel the throb of my heart in my throat, the threat of a sob. But I'm not going to lost it here. "Konner?" I say, with a trembling voice. I glance around, but he's standing with us, at Derrick's elbow, his eyes bright and sparkly, in shock. I raise my eyebrows. A look that says, *Well?*

He nods. One of those big up and down nods. Konner says *yes*.

And so do I. Well, almost. There's still one more thing.

Mr. B leans on the wall nearby, smiling, perplexed. "What did I say?"

"Something good." I glance at Derrick, who still looks floored, then back at Mr. B again. "Could Konner check out the game room?" I ask. "To give us a couple of minutes to talk?"

There's one more thing that could kill the whole deal.

"Absolutely." He pushes away from the wall. "Come on, Konner. Let's set you up."

A minute later, the teacher returns and waves us into the conference room. "What's up?" he says.

We sit around the too-big table. Too big for just the three of us. Derrick sits on the end, to my right, and the teacher sits across from me.

"I'm sure you have questions." Mr. B says.

Derrick gives me a wink. "Kristal comes with a list."

I smile and feel a bit warm, embarrassed. But he's right. I do. I tend to have lots of questions and I don't want to forget anything. But today I only have one question. "I need to know if you're really prepared to handle Konner."

Mr. B's sitting back from the table, leaning forward, his hands clasped between his legs. And he's listening to me. Without a trace of those cold detached stares I've grown to despise. He nods. "I've read his file. Go on. It's okay. Hit me."

Honesty. A scary proposition for me. I don't want to set Konner up to fail. Not here. Not anywhere else either. Which means I have to be candid. Blunt. It's something I realized at the end of the latest school year. A monstrous year in every respect.

I take a deep breath and take my time. "Konner is on the spectrum, yes. But the real illness we're struggling with is a mood disorder. His emotions are not only huge and intense, they're sudden and unexpected, too. Scary sometimes. And they spike over the smallest and most insignificant things." I pause, almost afraid of what he'll say when I'm done.

But, amazingly, he doesn't jump in and try to speak. He nods and waits, as if sensing I still have more to say.

"The best analogy I have is one that Konner's psychiatrist told us last week. It's this." I open my hands on the table. "His emotions are like a boiling pot of water, a pot that is going to overflow. To cool the pot and calm Konner down, you need to have ways to turn off the heat."

He nods and Derrick and I look at him.

"What if we had a hand signal?" Mr. B says. "Something Konner can use when he feels like he's bubbling up."

A shiver goes through me. A good one for a change. Derrick and I are the ones who are nodding now.

"I love that idea." I fold my hands together again.

"I've done it with other students. It helps. And we'll pick something the rest of the kids aren't going to recognize."'

Derrick rests an arm on the desk. "What if he can't? Use it, I mean? If he's too upset?"

Mr. B's body shakes with his nod. "I'm pretty good at reading kids. Like a sixth sense. Kids with emotional difficulties. If I think Konner is getting upset, I'll ask him to come to the conference room, or take him around outside for a walk."

"That won't disrupt the rest of the class?"

"My assistant can cover the class while we're out. That's why I love this setup so much."

A man with a plan. I can barely believe it. And not only that. A man who isn't afraid of what I just said.

I look at Derrick, who seems bemused.

"Okay." I say. "I think we're all in agreement then."

"Can I ask one thing?" Mr. B says. "Before you go?"

I'm instantly tense. I'm used to running on dread mixed with adrenaline. "Sure." There's always a catch, isn't there?

"Does Konner have time for a game of chess?"

Two weeks later, after a long and adventurous southerly drive to the Gulf, we splash in the gentle warmth of the sea. Waves that are perfect for boogie boarding. Konner lets out a muted shout, which I hear over the roll of the surf, then he turns and leaps up onto the board with a belly flop, his face alight. Derrick hoots and soars beside him, his shaved head rich and brown from the sun.

Konner glides onto the sand with a large uproarious laugh. Then he shoves back up to his feet again, holding the board. He splashes back in.

Thanks to a huge and silky sandbar, I'm standing out farther than either of them, to help Brennig avoid the waves, but I see one rolling straight for me.

"Uh oh!" I laugh.

Brennig goes stiff with worry beside me.

I grab him beneath the arms and scoop him into the air. He laughs, looking less nervous now, so I laugh too, so pleased to see him having some fun, so pleased that his screaming nightmares have stopped.

My eyes go back to Konner again. He jumps a wave and so does Derrick. The two of them fly. It's amazing to see how much fun he's having, and the rest of us, too, and I can't help but feel in awe of this moment.

It's a moment, I almost hate to say, that's possible because of those bubblegum pills.

Look at me. What an idiot, huh? I tried to fix my son with my hands, my cooking hands, and I flat-out failed. And maybe that's good, that was meant to be, because the weight of his illness, and trying to fix it, too, is washing away with every rocking sweep of the waves.

Konner lets out a giggling laugh and I lift Brennig over the wave. It's amazing. Konner's moods are infectious. The bad ones. Also the good ones, too. The fact

is, since he started on Lithium eight weeks ago, he's only

had two or three tantrums at home. The fewest we've seen.

Every day now he jokes or gives us a puzzle to figure out,

or quietly sits in the back of the car. Every day of this peace

is an absolute gift. And I feel the relief of his lighter moods,

like balloons gently tugging me up.

This is my son. Set free at last.

And this is our week. An entire vacation without

any battles. It's more than I could have hoped for after the

year we've been through. And the more I think of it, the

more I realize. If Konner hadn't had such a terrible year,

we'd never have found his great new home. And Mr. B.

All these things are simply. And truly. Miraculous.

And I wish I could live in this moment forever. But, as

truly hardened soldiers know, when one war seems to come

to an end, an entirely new one's about to blow up right in

your face.

Chapter 10

Open Wounds

The boys and me on one of my good days, 2015

I battled the monstrous dragon for years. Twelve long years. Something I hardly can fathom now. I looked in its eyes and endured its screams. I wrestled it down to the floor to keep it from hurting me. I cooked. I took it to doctor's appointments. I advocated in schools for it. And I honestly don't know how I did it all.

Well, I do. I'll be honest. I worked in a strength that wasn't my own. A divine strength. Because most days I barely was making it through.

But, now, curled on the couch, I've lost it. Konner is happy and flexible, free, most of the time, while I feel drained, scooped out, like a shell. With little to show for the last dozen years except for a calm and healthy son.

Except.

I know.

That's a monstrous choice of words I'm using. As if having a healthy agreeable son isn't worth the years of anguish and non-stop energy I poured into him. And it shows what a terrible funk I'm in.

The fire crackles and licks at the wood in the fireplace, but I shiver, cold. It's a cold that aches in my bones as if they've been molded out of icicles.

I'm wrapped in a thick and furry blanket, but I barely notice. Instead I think how empty I feel. How much time I've lost. My thirties, my youth. What do I have to show for my life?

It's Thanksgiving Day, which we'd normally spend with family. But Derrick and I are recuperating from a stomach virus, so there isn't going to be cooking today. Fortunately, his family dropped off some food. So the boys will stay fed, at any rate.

I hear the boys giggle upstairs, their laughter floating down to me. They're keeping themselves occupied, another one of those miracles, which is good since I can't do anything for them.

My stomach's starting to settle at last, but the virus isn't the worst thing I'm fighting off today. Neither is the exhaustion I feel. I'm tired in a way that sleep can't seem to reach anymore. It's something deeper, sicker, than that.

Derrick softly clears his throat. He sits across from me in his armchair, eyes on his tablet. He swipes the screen, turning the page in whatever home improvement magazine he's reading.

I stare at the fire. At the flames devouring the wood in the same way the monster seems to have devoured my life. I'm forty-two, as of a few weeks ago. Another birthday without a finished book to publish. That's how it feels.

You could jab me and say, hey, look, you helped your family through a tremendous ordeal. You slayed the dragon and freed your son. And, because of that, you freed your family along with him.

But I still have nothing to show for my life. A piece of wood snaps, and I twitch at the sound.

Derrick sets his tablet aside. "You okay, baby?"

I feel like I'm sinking through quicksand now. A thick wet sand that bleeds into a massive network of caves below. I'm sinking, barely able to breathe, too weak to struggle or even scream.

To be honest, part of me thinks I deserve to be sucked down there. I'm worthless. Weak. I have nothing to give.

"No," I finally say. "I'm not." But there's no relief in admitting the words. I slide my arms around me, cold, but it seems more like I'm trying to hold myself together. "I think I need to go to the doctor."

"Are you feeling worse?"

I'm finding it hard to meet his gaze. I'm ashamed of the sickness growing inside. "It's not this stupid stomach bug."

He frowns. "What is it?"

I struggle to breathe and to say the words. "I'm depressed, Derrick." It's an illness I've had a few times before, before we even started to date. But it's bad this time. Really bad. "I need to go in."

"Today?"

I push the blanket aside. "Tomorrow, I guess." I wobble a bit as I get to my feet. My legs feel weak. "I need to lie down." And I feel his worried eyes on my back as I leave the room.

I climb the stairs like a zombie, so hollow and cold inside, and fall into bed, to escape the pain the only way I seem to know how right now. To sleep for as long as I possibly can.

*

And I do, I sleep. For most of the year, I'm curled in bed, beneath the blankets, worse than ever, unable to

229

fight for myself at all. Despite the anti-depressants I'm on, I'm screaming inside. I've dropped into the cavernous dark and its icy water. I'm drowning in it, thrashing and trying to scream, alone.

Is this how Konner felt? I wonder, in the raging dark of that monster's belly? Because I've been swallowed by my own monster. And I don't even have to get up to go to school.

A door scrapes out. I open my eyes. Derrick emerges from his office, slowly, looking exhausted. My fault, I think. And I close my eyes, too tired to keep them open for long.

He shakes the bed as he sits beside me and rests his palm on top of my hip. When I'm able to open my eyes again, I see his lips moving quietly in some silent prayer.

Don't bother, I think, lashing out with an anger that frightens me. I've never felt so alone in my life. Alone with my husband sitting beside me.

"I don't like this," he says. There's a darkness around his eyes now and a huge invisible weight, too. A weight I've somehow shared with him and I can't take back. For months he's worked a long and mentally strenuous day, then come out of his office, tired, ordered takeout for us, then taken care of the boys from there.

I'm barely able to function at all.

There's nothing to say, so I don't. I'm lost. So devoid of strength I can barely move.

"I think you should switch," he says.

"My meds?" To what? I think.

"To Dr. Ruben."

I let out a long, exhausted sigh. "Too much money."

231

He shakes my hip. Gently. "Kristal."

I open my eyes.

"This doctor you're seeing? He isn't worth it. Konner was a really complex case. And Ruben helped him. Maybe something that worked for Konner will work for you."

The tears are hot and starting to fall. I've done this to us. Spent all our money on doctor's appointments and take-out food, and now I'm going to visit the priciest doctor I possibly could.

"Call him tomorrow," he says. "I don't care. Whatever it costs. We'll figure it out."

"Okay." My tears bleed into the pillow.

Do I tell him I don't want to live anymore? Do I tell him that?

"Mom?" Brennig stands at the open doorway. And Konner is quietly peering around behind him.

Derrick shoots me a look, to make sure I'm feeling up to talking to them.

I nod. Okay. I've barely checked on the boys today. Or the last few months. What kind of terrible mother am I?

He pushes up to his feet. "I'll order some dinner." He stops and looks at the boys. "Just a couple of minutes. Then let your mom rest."

Brennig leans over and kisses me on the forehead. In his sweet soft voice, he asks, "Would you like a massage?"

I don't. I don't really want to be touched. But he looks at me with those huge hopeful blue-gray eyes. And, so help me, I mumble, "Okay, baby."

He pulls the covers away from me.

Konner leans in to kiss my cheek. "Roll over?" he says.

I can barely move. I'm heavy. Concrete. But I force myself to untangle the knot I've been lying in, and I do as he says.

He works his thumbs into my back, while Brennig gently kneads my legs. My sweet, sweet boys. I've fought for them, for peace in the house, for so many years.

Now it's their turn to fight for me.

*

I pull up to the small historic train station that sits on the shores of the Hudson River. It's built entirely of chiseled gray stones and it feels a little bit castle-like. Only, it isn't a train station now.

I step out of the SUV and the April wind slaps my face. Painful and raw. It makes me grimace. I peer at the building, feeling nervous. It's owned now by a writing center, and I've signed up for their year-long novel writing class, something I don't feel up to yet, but something I think will be good for me, since it gets me out of the house. And writing.

I've taken the first two legs of the class, which runs in six-week-long increments, and today I'll get my instructor's comments on the first twenty pages of my book. Something that makes me feel queasy inside and, yeah, a little bit naked, too. But I force myself to close the car door, with my fingers hooked through the leather tote bag over my shoulder.

I push my way through the glass front door, into the spacious rectangular room. Along the rear wall, tall glass doors face the train lines in and out of the city, and the cold gray river that's just beyond. A huge wooden table fills half the room, and the seats are all filled, except for mine. I'm the last one in.

And I'm feeling exposed, walking in by myself. It would be easier to stay in bed all day, to hide and sleep, but I'm pushing myself. I'm trying at least. Trying to do something productive and therapeutic with my time.

A tough but chatty redhead named Jo sits next to the last remaining seat and she smiles at me. "Hey," I say and I slip into the folding chair. I wave or nod to some of the others. It's a bit of a drive for me to get here. Almost an hour. So I'm usually the last to arrive.

I find it hard to speak very much, let alone try to be heard over everyone else who's talking. I've lost something since my illness began. I've lost myself and my confidence, and all that's left of me is this shell.

Tammy, our teacher, is a published author and smiles at us with this wonderful delighted energy. She's wearing a deep magenta jacket with a flowery scarf of reds and blacks. The office isn't available, so she's going to call us into the kitchen, off to one side, and meet with us each, one by one.

She gestures to Jo, and the two of them head to the kitchen to talk.

My stomach flutters. I peek at the exit, wanting to leave, to just chicken out. I'm not sure I can take any bad news today. *Coward,* I think. Don't you want to improve your writing, get published? So I scribble down some questions about my book, talking to the others occasionally, but only if someone says my name. I've gotten way too reticent, I think. I've been so focused on communicating Konner's needs for so long, I've forgotten how to interact with people for fun.

"Kristal?" Tammy waves on my right from the hallway.

My heart shudders at the sound of my name and I stand and head to the open doorway that stands to the right. Tammy is already sitting inside, with the electrical lines for the trains visible through the window behind her.

It's a tiny space, just room enough for the two of us, in addition to the fridge and sink and shelves. She's holding an envelope on her lap and she flashes me a bright and cheerful smile. "I just have to tell you," she says. "what a wonderful writer you are. But I hope you know that."

Sure, I think, and I sit in the chair across from her. I don't think much of my writing these days, so of course I assume others don't either. It's a terrible state of mind to be in.

She pulls my manuscript out of the yellow envelope, with a page of typewritten comments on top. She taps the stack with her fingertips. "I can see why that agent at the conference you attended asked to see the rest of your manuscript."

I hate the reminder. It was something that happened two years ago. Forever ago. An agent had read my very first page and loved the writing, and wanted to see the entire book. But I just got…stuck. I couldn't rework the manuscript in order to send it to her.

I picture a thumb and hand planted against my forehead. *Loser*, I think.

"Second," she says and she tugs at her scarf. "I have some ideas about what you can do to make this work. The big one is this: You need to slow down. You don't have to give us non-stop action the whole way along. Slow down and get into character. Show why your characters are stuck where they are and hint at the things that are going to happen."

239

I nod. Okay. That makes sense to me. But I'm struggling with a terrible writer's block. I don't have a clue how to slow things down. And I tell her that.

She clasps her painted fingers together. "If you'd like, I can give you the name of someone who can read your entire manuscript and tell you what they think needs done. They'd charge a fee, of course, but it's worth it."

No way, I think. I'm not showing anyone, a single person, my whole tangled up manuscript. I'm not going to embarrass myself. "Can I think about that?"

"Of course!" she says.

But I won't. I know that. I know how awful my writing is now, while I'm feeling like this. Exhausted and all knotted up inside. And I've had enough disappointment to last me a very long time.

I close the car door after class, relieved to be out of the spotlight again, and my cell phone rings. "Laurel?" I say. It's twelve now, but it's three hours earlier in Arizona, and Laurel doesn't usually call this early.

She pauses. "Dad's sick." And her voice is strange.

The other women walk in a group past my windshield, and I force myself to wave at them. "What's wrong?" I say.

"Pneumonia." Her voice is quiet, restrained.

I don't like it at all. I close my eyes. "Do I need to come out?" And I know whatever she says next is going to change my entire life.

She sighs. "Yes. I think you'd better."

*

It's a week later and I've barely slept. I've stayed with my dad in his ICU room around the clock and listened

241

to the awful hiss of the respirator breathe for him. I've jumped from my little windowseat bed in the middle of the night whenever he moaned, confused by the sedation and painkillers they were giving him. And I sat by his side, holding his hand.

But all of that is over now.

The machines and the tubes are quiet, off, for the first time all week. So quiet I wish I could turn them back on. The nurse, a man who is tall and incredibly quiet-spoken, switches off the lights for us and leaves, casting the bed and the room in a weak brownish glow. My dad's lying with his head to the side, his mouth still open, looking as if he's sleeping. He's not.

Pneumonia, they said. Complicated by scarring in his lungs, they said. Whatever it was, he could no longer breathe on his own. And he's gone.

This place couldn't be real, I think. None of this is. But I'm holding my daddy's hand in mine and resting my head on the top of it, too. It's cold, his hand, and it's pale. Not gray. Just cold and heavy and colorless. Lacking his usual pale-pink flush.

My grip hardens. It's mine, this hand. My daddy's hand. And I'm squeezing it hard and possessively, trying to hold him, keep him, weight him to life. To earth. Weight him to me.

Laurel sits slumped on the other side, her head propped on my dad's shoulder, and I think maybe she's slipped off to sleep. If so, that's good. Forgetting is good. Or that's what I think while I'm sitting here.

My mom is sitting next to her, looking rumpled and frail. "Here," she says.

My head comes up.

My mom's face is open, tender. As I watch, she shifts her hand beneath the blanket and slides it from dad's thigh all the way up to his chest. "Here." She leans over him, her eyes glassy and bright with tears. "He's warmest right here."

I'm tired, shaky-tired by now, and my eyes are burning with tears again. My hand is moving all on its own, tucking under the blanket and brushing his ribs on the way, sliding along the thin ridiculous fabric people seem to enjoy calling a gown.

My hand stops, heavy, exhausted, on top of his chest, and I feel it now. The *warmth* in his chest. Like he hasn't quite left.

I lean in close and try to whisper to him, but my brain and mouth feel stuffed with sour and rotten leaves and the words don't come. So tired. So warm. And I lean on his chest, and curl up my feet on top of the chair, and close my eyes for as long as I can. As long as that tall quiet

nurse will let me.

*

His loss lingers everywhere, and the darkness of it

preys on me, especially at times when I'm feeling frail.

And alone. Depressed.

It's a damp summer night. The windows are open

and the air feels heavy and harder to breathe. But I try to

watch a movie with Konner and Derrick. Brennig's away at

a friend's tonight and Konner's picked out his favorite kind

of movie. Horror, of course. I make it about three-quarters

of the way through, through the heart-stopping jump-scares

and quick jolts of noise, before the huge grinning thing in

my head opens its cavernous mouth and swallows me

whole.

And, just that quick, I'm drowning in a lake of depression again. Thrashing. Screaming. It's too much to take.

I leave our flickering TV room without a word and walk to the kitchen. I'm empty except for the whispers I hear. The ones that say how worthless I am and how pointless it is to live when I'm going to die anyway. We're all going to die. Life looks so much different, darker, now that I've lost someone I love, and it doesn't make a bit of difference that I'm Christian and believe that life goes on after earth. I'm too focused on the pain that's screaming inside, too consumed, too desperate to make it stop.

I move to the sliding door that's open and sit on the tiles in front of the screen, just wanting to touch and smell something real. I lean forward over my crossed legs, with my nose practically touching the screen. A light rain is falling outside in the dark and the air smells soft. Through

246

the screen I can feel the wet of the rain as it hits the deck and bounces back up. In my mind I imagine the rain is blood.

And I sense something awful lurking nearby. Not Derrick or Konner. They're watching the movie. It's something I see through a dark inner eye, inside my brain. It's pale-faced, hooded. And it stands to my left, grinning at me.

I shiver, freaked. And I wish I were dead. Just free of this terrible empty ache and the inner screams nobody hears. I don't want to die and go to heaven, or anywhere good. I don't deserve it. I just want die. To cease to exist. To feel nothing at all forever and ever. A very un-Christian-like death to be sure. And I sense the grinning thing that's stooping over me now wants the same thing. It wants me dead, too.

I hug myself, and tell myself, no, not to think like that. It's just a figure of my imagination, I'm sure, because of the movie. Or maybe it's the depression personified, goading me, wanting me to do it. But whatever it is, I can't let myself give into it.

Can I? I'm tired. So tired.

"Everything okay?" Derrick stops at the fridge and fills his glass.

I turn my head, still hugging myself, still tied in a knot. And I'm sure my expression looks hopeless, pained. There's no masking any of it.

He sets down the glass and crouches beside me, down on one knee. "Feeling depressed?"

I stare out the screen into the dark. "The pain's too much. I don't want to live with it anymore. I'm tired of it. I'm tired of living. I'm sorry. I am."

"Kristal."

I glance at him.

His eyes are sharp and worried. "Are you thinking about hurting yourself?"

I shrug. How do you answer that?

His hand is fisted on top of his thigh and his voice is brusque. "I thought you loved me more than that."

I press my palm to the cold tile to steel myself against his words. "I do," I say. I've hurt him, this man who loves me so much.

"Then why would you want to hurt yourself?"

I look away and try to think of the words to describe how I feel inside. "It's like I can't feel you at all," I say. "All I feel is *me*. All I feel is the *dark*. It fills me up and it hurts and I'm screaming and nobody hears. It's too much to take. I want it to stop."

When he doesn't respond, I turn my head. His eyes are damp. "I never realized that's how—" He lowers his head.

I lift my hand and slide my knuckles along his jaw. Its smooth and shaved until I reach the tickle of his dark and graying goatee. It's the jaw of this man who loves me so much. "I'm sorry," I say. If I hurt myself, I'll destroy this man. I'll destroy my boys. How could I possibly do that to them.

He lifts his gaze. "Will you call the doctor tomorrow? Please?"

I sigh. "Yes. Okay. I'll call." And when I look past him, I sense that the grinning creature is gone.

*

A few weeks later, I stare out Dr. Ruben's window, at the wet gray skies and the way the maple trees twist and try to escape the rain.

I'm crazy. Nuts. That's what I think. And I feel the stigma following me wherever I go. I'm less than, I think. Less than everyone else around. And the fact that Konner suffered like this ahead of me has absolutely no bearing on anything. I'm the mom. I'm supposed to be better. Stronger. Saner somehow.

But the meds are as hard to pick for me as they were for Konner.

The doctor leafs through the stack of papers that sits on his lap. The results of all my genetic testing. To see which meds might help me most.

He's a small and unassuming man with a mild accent, but he's sharp and thorough in his approach. "The problem," he says, "is your sensitivity to so many medications on this list." He sets the papers aside on a shelf. "I'm not sure how much this list is helping."

I'm kneading my hands on top of my lap. "Is this normal?" I say. "Taking so long to get some relief? Because I can't, I can't bear to think how long—" But I can't finish. The tears bubble out. I can't keep going like this anymore.

On top of all that, I miss my dad. I miss being able to call him and ask his advice on things. I miss his voice.

"This is absolutely *not* normal," the doctor says. "You are very sick and I'm going to help you. Okay? Yes? At the same time, it's not exactly unexpected either."

"You're talking about Konner."

"Precisely." He holds up his open palms. "As I've said before, when a child like yours, with so many issues, gets well at last…the parents who've suffered along with him are finally free to—" He spreads his hands as if letting a few things flutter out.

"Fall apart."

"It's a very real form of PTSD. Yours is complicated by the fact that you cannot tolerate so many medications that might otherwise help. Instead they simply make you worse. So. Now. Let me ask you this. Have you heard of something called TMS?"

A bell seems to ding in my head. "Actually, I'm amazed you just said that because my mom saw a news story about it last week. It's based on MRI technology?"

"It is."

"Do you think it might actually work for me?"

The doctor's eyebrows go up and he nods. "I do," he says. "It's meant for patients who aren't responding to medication. And it has some wonderful results as well. I

253

know someone in your area who's doing it. He's good. I'll give him a call."

And just that fast, some hope appears on the horizon again.

*

The room is a dark and relaxing green, and rectangular, a lot like a spa. In it sit two reclining chairs, padded, each one facing its own TV. Behind each chair stands a tall piece of machinery. White. Attached to a large digital screen. It's a machine that produces a magnetic field, which it pulses directly into the brain where a person's mood is regulated. Transcranial Magnetic Stimulation, it's called. Or TMS.

I sit in the chair farthest from the door. "Will it work, do you think?" I lift my feet and lean against the padded headrest. It's not unlike a dentist's chair. "For me, I mean."

The doctor, tall with dark ruffled hair, stands with his hands behind his back, while the attendant, a girl, moves around the chair and readies things.

The doctor wears a wide and easy smile. "Like I said, the research shows just how effective it is. The bulk of patients still have complete remission of symptoms after a year." He lifts the folder he was clutching behind him. "That stack of papers you filled out last week? They show you're a very good candidate. Wonderful, in fact. I know you'll respond."

I let out the breath I was holding. "Okay. I just really, desperately need this to work." And I can't help it. I'm skeptical that nobody's talking about it, when the research is there and when insurance actually covers it.

"I hear the same thing from our other patients." He slowly nods. "And I've seen them walk away changed.

Well. I can't guarantee it. Of course, I can't. But I'm very optimistic that this will turn things around for you."

I sigh. "Thank you for saying that."

He hands me a pair of earplugs sealed in plastic bag. I roll them between my fingers and wiggle them into my ears. Next, he gives me a TV remote and shows me how to navigate through the channels on it.

"Will it hurt?" I say.

"You shouldn't have much discomfort, no. A prickly sensation. Maybe a slight headache afterward. If it hurts more than that, just raise your hand. We'll come out and lower the current a bit."

The attendant straps my head into place and I roll my eyes to look at the doctor.

He raps on his dark feathered hair. "Think of it as a doorknocker. Knocking on things and waking them up in the cerebellum."

"Good things, I hope."

He laughs. "I forgot. You're a writer. One of those creative types." He moves to the door. "Well, save the scary ideas for your books. There's nothing scary to see in here."

I give him a wry smile. "Got it."

He waves and steps out.

The attendant pushes the large magnet into my hair. It clicks into place. Then she side-steps out of my field of vision to tap the screen and adjust some settings. For another minute, she double-checks all her measurements, then she says, "How is it?"

"Fine. I'm good."

She waves at me and dims the lights. A moment later, the hammering sound of the magnet starts and I feel a prickling warmth on my scalp. I hit the button to stream a scary sci-fi series, but I somehow feel like the actress in here, starring in my own sci-fi flick. All I hope is there won't be too many more unexpected twists.

*

Three months later, I pull up our long and curving drive and park outside the closed garage. I sit behind the wheel a moment, taking stock of the way I feel. So clear-headed. And energetic. Not perfect yet. I still struggle with lots of anxious thoughts. But I don't feel imprisoned by pain anymore, and I don't entertain those sick, dark thoughts of hurting myself.

The TMS is responsible for at least fifty percent of my healing, on top of the meds the doctor prescribed, two mood stabilizers, an anti-depressant, and something to give me some energy. Little do I know it, but in less than a year, I'll be dropping two meds that I'll no longer need and feeling the best that I have in years. All thanks to some creatively repurposed tech.

The garage door rumbles up on its own. Inside, Konner stands in the opening to the kitchen, holding the door. I wave to him. He closes the door and pads outside in his stockinged feet.

I roll the window down for him, trying to decide whether to leave the car out or not. There isn't much on the agenda today. School won't start for another week. Maybe I should take the boys to a movie.

Konner peers in, hands resting on the window frame, and looks around. "Hello," he says. It's almost as if he expects to see something inside with me. Maybe the depression that's dragged me around for the last few years? The grinning thing? Guess what? It's gone.

"What's up?" I say. I twist the key and the car shudders off.

"How did your TMS go?" he says.

I nod. "Good. I'm feeling good. In fact, Dr. Ruben thinks it might be helpful for you one day."

"Okay," he says, looking around. But he's holding back, talking much slower than usual. "Mom?"

"You okay, bud?"

"Can I ask you something?" Konner says.

"Of course. What's up?"

He gives me a look that's uncomfortable. Anxious. "Did I make you sick?"

"Sick? Step back." I open the door and sit on the seat sideways. "What makes you say that?"

He shrugs. "You got the depression after…me."

"And your issues. I did."

"So I made you sick." He drops his head.

"Come here." I open my arms to him. He steps in close and I lean forward to hug him, hard. "It's not your fault. And it's not my fault. I just got sick."

I feel him nodding his head against me.

"Sometimes a thing just happens, okay? But it takes a bunch of things to set that thing off. Genetics. Stress. Exhaustion. Food. Lots of things." I pull back so I can see him better. "Now tell me the truth. Did you have autism on purpose?"

"No!" He laughs at that.

"Well then, it's not your fault. Got it?"

He nods and starts to turn away, but a bee flies past his hand and he jerks. I stow that away for another day.

He's afraid of bees, but they're starting to freak him out more and more.

"Hey, Konner?" I say.

He ducks and waves his arms and the bee finally zooms away. When he turns around, he's out of breath.

"You okay?" I laugh.

He's looking around. Looking for bees.

"I just wanted to say, good things always come from the bad. You know?"

He shakes his head. He doesn't know.

"I know how it feels to be overwhelmed by emotion now." I reach for his arm and give it a squeeze. "It helps me understand you a lot better. And everything you had to go through, too."

He darts at my face, so fast I flinch, but all he does is peck at my cheek. "I love you, Mom." He turns and races around the door.

I laugh. "Yeah? I love you more."

"Most!" he says and he flies inside. The door stops, halfway closed. He peers back out. "I'm going to have some ice cream now!"

I laugh. "Sweet." And it is sweet. But sometimes the briefest moments in life are sweeter.

So what helped me get through the worst of the depression, aside from the meds and the TMS? Prayer. I can see that more and more each day. No matter how much I wished I was dead, I felt some sort of restraining force holding me back. And, so, here I am. My writing gave me a reason to keep going, too, no matter how tough it was at the time. And my two closest friends, Derrick and my sister,

Laurel, listened and loved and spoke the tough words when they needed to.

I'm alive today because of these things. And so many more.

*

Derrick steers the SUV onto the grass across the street from a large sprawling Colonial, and parks it between a pickup truck and a Mercedes Benz. I step out onto the grass in heels and a black sleeveless dress. I shift my gaze across the street, where couples are strolling up a short drive beside the house and handing tickets to a woman there. It's one of first few days I've felt well enough to attend an event.

Let alone something special like this.

Konner slams the door behind me.

"Ready?" I say.

He shrugs but doesn't answer me. And that could be either good or bad. He fans away a bug near his head. He's never liked being around lots of people.

I want to reach out and fix his collar, which is starting to curl up on one side, but I manage to keep my hands to myself. He's handsome in his blue long-sleeve shirt and khaki pants. Just about the best I've seen him, in fact.

He grimaces at me. I've stared too long.

We cross the road as a family and head to the bubbly woman who's taking tickets.

"Hi!" she says. "You're Konner's mom! I've seen you out at the farm."

Konner with his favorite horse, Cody, 2016

"Hey," I say, feeling relieved. "I remember you now." I was feeling out of place, to be honest, at the entrance to the wide twinkling yard. The fact is we were invited to attend this gala for free. It's a fundraiser for the horse farm where Konner rides twice a week. "Alex said our names are on the list."

"Oh!" The woman's eyes light up, and she finds our names. "So Konner," she says, looking at him. "Which horse do you ride?"

"Cody," he says.

"Cody's the best." She winks. "Have fun."

I can tell he doesn't want to be here. He's bored. And anxious, too. And he's looking around for flying things. But it's for a good cause. The farm where he rides is a sanctuary that rescues horses, then uses those horses to help heal people. People like Konner who've been so impacted by the horses and the way they feel when they ride.

We wander around the backyard, playing ping-pong, eating yummy snacks off plates, and visiting a couple of the horses stabled on the property there. Soon, a couple of women head toward us. Gianna, the owner of the horse sanctuary, whose dark hair's loose of its bun today, but kept in check under a black cowboy hat, and Lexi, who paid for our tickets tonight, and who's wearing a black sparkling blouse and matching boots.

Lexi's dark wavy hair shimmers like her shirt and she winks at Konner. "Can we ask you a favor?"

Konner gives her a blank stare. Neither good nor bad. "What kind of favor?"

Gianna squats in the grass in front of him, looking up at him from under her hat. "Could you stand up there—" She turns and points at a multi-tiered deck. "And tell everyone how riding a horse from the rescue has changed your life?"

Zinger. Wow. I bite my lip, worried.

He shrugs. "I guess."

Lexi beams. "We'll be right beside you." She holds out her hand and he slips his own into hers. He's only met her a handful of times, but he's amazingly comfortable with her, for sure. He walks with the women across the grass.

"Wow," says Brennig. "Isn't he nervous?"

I peer at Derrick who simply raises his eyebrows, surprised.

"Guess not, kiddo," I say. "But I am."

People stream to the large round tables with twinkling candles and tablecloths. It's going to be a relaxed dinner at least, buffet style, but we sit first and wait for Konner to speak.

I'm breathless, looking at him up there, standing between the two dark-haired women.

Gianna thumbs her hat back a bit and smiles into the microphone. "What a gorgeous evening, everyone! Thank you for coming!" And she chats about the sanctuary a bit and thanks everyone for helping to raise money for the horses there. "But before you eat, a special young man named Konner Johnson would like to tell you how Cody, a horse at our sanctuary, has changed his life."

There's whistling. Applause. And I keep a hand pressed to my mouth. Awed, and afraid. Very afraid. With a glance around, I estimate 50 plus people are watching. Watching a kid who hates to be watched. Watching a kid who's flipped out for much smaller reasons than this. Not in a while. But recently enough that I have to worry.

Gianna hands Konner the microphone. And he stands there, looking uncomfortable, for a long, long time. So long I start to rise from my seat.

Then he opens his mouth. "When I started to ride," Konner says, "I used to get pretty upset with Cody. Upset she wouldn't cooperate and do what I was telling her to do." He paused, letting us think about that.

"But then, over time, as Cody and I really got used to each other, all that changed." He shook his head. "Now it isn't me riding a horse anymore. Cody and I are partners instead."

He glances at me, where I sit and watch. "More than that, when I ride, it feels like Cody and I are *one.*"

My eyes blur with hot tears. Did he just say that? For a kid who couldn't communicate his needs for years and years, I'm stunned at how articulate he is. In front of a crowd.

Another woman at the table leans in, older, wearing a gauzy blouse, not knowing Konner's history. "An amazing young man," she says. "You must be so proud."

The tears bubble onto my cheeks.

"Well, I guess that just about says it all."

I laugh. "Yeah." I swipe my face. "It really does. I'm so, so proud."

"Thank you." I whisper my prayer out loud.

Chapter 11

The Monster Rears its Ugly Head

But my fight for Konner isn't over. I sit at home, still trying to write, when the phone rings.

Luckily, up until now, Konner's done fairly well at his new middle school. Until today.

"Hello?" I say, not really sure what to expect from the call.

"Mrs. Johnson. Hi. This is Nurse Brenda." She's a tough but tender older woman whose husband passed away a few months before.

Crap, I think. I haven't even showered yet. I went right to work. Am I going to have to pick him up? "Is Konner okay?"

"Well, he's not sick or anything, sweetie. But he came here upset. He says a teacher's aide wouldn't let him

Konner wearing his beekeeper outfit to get the mail, 2017

cross a road outside near the parking lot, even when he told her he has permission. The two of them got into a bit of a spat. So she sent him to me."

I hear somebody mumble behind her. Not Konner's voice. But deep, like a man's.

"Hang on," she says. And her voice is muffled and farther away. "Konner," she says. "He's just going to call the office to let them know you're here."

I hear a scream. "No!"

Then a grunt and a shout and a muffled sound, like fabric sliding over the phone's receiver. The line clunks and finally goes dead.

I fly up the stairs, toss the phone onto the bathroom rug, and jump in the shower. Ten minutes later the phone rings and I'm standing, clothed, with my hair dripping down the back of my shirt. "Yes, hello?" I say.

"Nurse Brenda again." She sighs. "Okay. Sorry to hang up on you. Konner didn't want the security guard to call the office, so he tried to wrestle the walkie-talkie out of his hand. When he couldn't do that, he bit him." So that was the other voice in the room. A security officer.

I cover my face. It's déjà vu. It feels like the day when Konner lost it at his last school, when the school resource/police officer was in the room, too.

"Is the man okay?"

She pauses, and it sounds like the man is still in the room. "Yes, he's okay. It didn't break through."

"Well, that's good. I'm relieved. And this doesn't mean what Konner did was right, but he really can't handle having more than one adult with him at a time when he's upset."

"Oh," she says, sounding surprised. "I'm sorry. I wasn't sure what to do."

I stand there, as if I've been struck by lightning. I've talked to his teacher about things he can do when Konner's upset, but have I really talked to anyone else? Or am I simply assuming they all know what to do already, since they happen to work for a special-ed school?

I'm kicking myself mentally. So stupid, I think, not to do this before.

I shake my head, and feel cold drips soaking my shirt. "You wouldn't. It's okay. I'm still figuring out what to do myself. But, I wonder, could you transfer me to the principal, please? I think I probably have a better way of handling this type of thing in the future."

*

I'm nervous, with a loud hammering heart. The principal, a dark and genial woman who's wearing a speckled ankle-length skirt, leads me back to the conference room where a roomful of teachers and staff members sit. A dozen or more. Including Mr. B who smiles with his bright and usual warmth.

Normally, I'd be here to listen to *them*. Today, they're here to listen to me.

I blink, shaky with stage fright but I manage to smile, though it feels more like I'm stretching my lips. It's been years since I had to present in front of a group of people. Years since I've felt sure of myself, healthy and strong, and confident in what I'm going to say. But today I need to be strong for Konner. He's the reason I'm here. So I focus instead on what I must do.

I sit in the last remaining chair and drop my purse on the floor beside me. "Thanks so much for having me," I say. I belong here, I think. I belong here for Konner. In my hands, I clutch the pages I'd like to review this morning.

I clear my throat. Everyone's eyes are focused on me and I hate the nervous warble in my voice as I start to speak. "We're here, of course, because Konner had an incident last week. And it led him to bite a security guard."

278

I smooth the pages out on the table in front of me, and lower my eyes every once in a while to recall the list I need to review.

But first, I say, "Konner is responsible for his actions. He is. With that said, I think there's another way we can deal with Konner when he's upset. A way to deescalate things before they get to the point they did."

People are nodding and watching me. Great.

"Think of it like this. When Konner's upset, he's steaming like a pot of very hot water." I lift one hand. "Whatever you say or do at that time can help him cool down or make him boil over." I lower my hand then raise it again.

"So, so true." Mr. B nods, looking around with his pale blue eyes.

I'm glad what I'm saying is ringing a bell. "I'd like to tell you a little about Konner and give you some practical steps you can follow to cool him down if it comes to that."

I feel myself flush. *Mental illness*, I think. But it has to be said. "Konner's on the autism spectrum, as some of you know, but he also has a mood disorder. What that means is he feels emotion much more strongly than other children do, and he can't regulate his moods on his own. They go up and down and all over the place. Especially when he's feeling upset."

I hold my hands tightly on top of my lap. "Before I go on, and talk about some things you can do to help him, do you have any questions?"

A hand goes up. It's the wrinkled hand of an older woman. Nurse Brenda, I realize. Since she and I have met a couple of times.

"Brenda?" I say. My gut twists since she was there during the incident.

But she gives me a sweet and interested smile. "This is so helpful," she says, "so thank you for that. I just wondered what types of things tend to set Konner off?"

I lay my fingers on the edge of the table, holding on for support. "That's a great question," I say. "It can be something tiny, like a repetitive sound that bothers him, or having too many people in the room, or listening to other people talk about him. But one of the common things that sets him off is simply *change*." I spread my hands. "Holidays, for instance. Or the start or end of the school year. Or a simple changeup to his daily routine. Like having a substitute teacher, for instance."

I lower my hands to the table again. "I should probably tell you that Konner is very rules-driven, too. If he's told he can cross the street outside near the parking lot, then he isn't allowed, well, you see how things started to escalate last week."

Brenda lifts her chin, her mouth open, with one of those aha looks on her face. "I see. Okay. Yes, I get it now."

I nod. "It's a lot. And some of these things are hard to foresee. And we certainly can't prevent them all. But I have some things I think will help."

A piece of hair tickles my face so I tuck it back behind my ear. "First. Mr. B's developed a hand signal Konner can use when he's feeling upset. As a warning that he's starting to feel upset."

Mr. B's nodding.

"It would be great if everyone here knew that signal. As a start anyway."

I move one of my papers aside to see what I've listed on page two. "Second," I say. "Don't ask him too many questions at first or overwhelm him with lots of people. Give him time and space to think and calm down. Unless, of course, safety for him or others around him are a main concern.

"Third. Let's come up with a list of 'safe people' for Konner. People he feels comfortable with who can help him when he's feeling upset. And let's designate other 'safe places,' like the conference room, the nurse's office, places like that where Konner can go until he calms down.

Brenda sticks up her hand. "I'd be happy to be a safe person for Konner."

"Thank you." I nod, feeling relieved. "I know he feels really comfortable with you." I glance down at my sheet again. "Okay. Fourth point. Give him some time to walk around until he's feeling less agitated.

"And fifth. When he's ready to talk, listen. Give him a chance to be heard first and to tell his side of the story to you.

"And last. Feel free to call me, of course. Just not in front of Konner, please, and not on speaker. Konner is easily embarrassed when people talk about him, and all it will do is make things worse." I've reached the end of my type-written notes.

"So I guess that's it." I peer up from my long and crazy list of behavioral interventions for Konner, afraid I'm giving them work to do, work they'll be unhappy about. When I look around at everyone, though, they're nodding and murmuring, appreciatively.

The principal leans forward onto the table, arms crossed. "I wish every parent would do this for us."

Really? I think. It never even occurred to me to *school* the school on the best things that work for my own

284

child. I figured they were just typical things. "I'm sorry it wasn't earlier," I say. "It wasn't until last week that I realized I might know some things worth telling you."

She lifts a hand, waving that off. "This makes our lives so much easier. I think I can speak for everyone here." She looks around and the others are nodding. "Thank you so much." And that's when I finally understand. These might be common sense things to me, as Konner's mother, but they're customized tactics for people who aren't as familiar with him.

I may no longer be an expert in corporate writing, I think. But I'm an expert in Konner. And from now on, I'm going to be clear and carefully deliberate when sharing my son's needs with other people.

*

High school starts innocently enough. It's Konner's first day. Ninth grade. Wow. At a wonderful place recommended to us by his doctor again. It's the smallest, most intimate setting he's had, at six students to a class, plus a teacher and aide. And it's far less likely to overstimulate Konner than any other school he's been to so far, but with lots of the perks a full high school has. What makes it even more special, though, is his music class.

He walks in the door at home with a smile and shoves some sheets of music at me. "Here. Look. I'm learning piano."

"You are?!" I say.

"It's a song called Für Elise. You'll like it."

I look at the sheets, amazed. First day. And he's learning piano. "I love it!" I say. "Remember that old keyboard we have?"

Konner's eyes widen. "I forgot about that!"

A friend of my dad's gave it to us when they moved a while back. Other than a little furious pounding, the kids barely used it. "It's still in the basement. Want me to bring it up to your room?"

He clasps his hands and jumps up and down.

A few minutes later, I'm plugging it into his bedroom outlet. "So how was gym?"

"Don't ask." His voice is tense and clipped.

My lips pull back in a grimace. "Were you able to go outside?"

"Duh." A bit of the old Konner leaks out of him. Or typical teenager attitude. I'm not really sure.

"That's not a nice way to talk, bud. Is that yes or no?"

"Too many bees." For the last few months, his fear of bees has skyrocketed into a phobia. And by that, I mean, he refuses to go outside at all.

Oh boy, I think. I thought we'd gotten through all the craziness, but the bug situation is getting worse. And, of course, there's absolutely no rationalizing with him. "I'll call the school."

I've already prepped the school about it, but now that it looks like gym is an issue, we're going to need a workaround. Luckily for Konner, the school has a small indoor gym, with a treadmill and bike and some free weights. Hopefully they'll let him use that for now.

But how long will they let him do his own thing before it starts to affect his grade?

Eight months later, on a bright spring day, he sits in the front passenger seat of our SUV and won't get out. The side of his face is hard, pale and immovable, like the foundation our home is sitting on. And he sits like a statue, ignoring the way I'm pleading with him.

It's warm outside, despite the fact that it's only April, a gorgeous day in a month with surprisingly little rain. Something the insects seem to love. I stand on the other side of his window on a patch of grass. Ahead is the indoor horse arena. But the idea of riding indoors doesn't seem to coax him out either. Too many flies in there, he says.

Samantha stands back to give me some room.

"Can't you just try?" I say. "Please? For a few minutes?" I bend at the waist to peer inside, but he won't turn his face to look at me.

289

Apiphobia. Or, that's what the doctor's calling it. A debilitating fear of bees. Though he's also afraid of flies, mosquitoes, gnats, you name it. He literally runs from the house to the car, and then back again. It's as if a bee is about to tear off a chunk off his flesh and turn him into some mindless, grotesque stumbling thing. Or is that what the bees have already achieved?

I tap on the window, twice with my nail, to make sure he's listening. "Samantha has an old riding hat with netting around it. Would you like to try it?"

His eyes roll in my direction. He shakes his head.

I blow out a breath, frustrated and turn away. Samantha's playing with the hat she brought, twisting the netting between her fingers.

"I don't know what else to do," I say. "It's the worst he's been."

"No worries," she says. "I'm sorry he's stuck feeling like this. Mind if I try?"

"I'd appreciate it." I step aside.

Samantha steps to the car. "Hey, Konner." She gives him a wave. "Would you like to ride Cody with me? I could sit behind you?"

He looks at her for a long moment, then shakes his head.

"Cody really misses you." She's his favorite horse, and he really has a connection with her.

He speaks through the door. "There are flies in there."

"How about this? I'll spray Cody with the natural repellant we use. I'll spray you, too. Then you and I can ride from here all the way down to the barn by the parking lot. How about that? Your mom can meet us, and you'll hop right back in the car again."

He doesn't look sure, but he doesn't look completely opposed to it either. And a few minutes later, he's perched on the horse, sitting slightly hunched, holding the reins, with Samantha behind him.

I stand at the top of the hill and watch, unable to breathe, both of my hands pressed to my mouth. She did it, I thought. She got him outside, and up on the horse. One of those little victories that will lead to an even bigger one. I think. I hope.

But, no, as soon as I pick him up, he panics getting into the car. And he says he's not sure about riding again.

*

"Okay," I say. "But you have to do it. The doctor said so." I pull that quote out of the far and distant past. Always blame it on the doctor, I think. And, for once, I can.

"He didn't say that," Konner says.

"Oh yes, he did. He called it chronic exposure therapy. For phobias. He said you need to go outside a little bit more each day, to get used to the bees."

"I'm not going to do that," he says.

"Listen. You're going to wear long pants and long-sleeved shirts, then you'll wear your beekeeper's hat and suit on top of that."

"I'm not going out."

"You have to, Konner. I need the mail."

He looks at me, dour.

"Don't worry," I say. "You'll be safe in your suit."

293

Five minutes later, stalling, reluctant, he's suited up. "The doctor didn't say this."

"He did."

He opens the front door and lets me follow him onto the porch, my phone in hand. It's not his fault, but he walks almost robotically in that big white suit, and I snap a couple of pictures while he isn't looking. Sorry. I did.

He manages to go all the way down, get the mail, and come halfway up until he starts to freak out.

"What's wrong?" I call.

"A bee! It landed right on my arm."

I hurry down the driveway to meet him and check him over. "Did it sting you?" I say.

"It almost did!" He darts for the kitchen door and slams it.

When I'm back inside, I find his beekeeper's hat on the floor and he's stomping up the steps to his room. "I'm not going back outside!" he says. "Or wearing that stupid costume again!"

A few days later, at his riding lesson, he refuses to get on a horse again, too. And this time, Samantha and I both are out of creative ideas.

*

I literally, honestly, don't know what to do. Nothing works. And it's almost as if we're in prison again. Konner in his own self-imposed cell, and the rest of us in our adjoining cells, practically unable to leave the house.

And then, a month later, we finally get a glimpse of a possible cure. It's early September, and Konner's first week of tenth grade, and another gym class he won't attend. Konner sits out in the doctor's quiet waiting room, while I sit in Dr. Ruben's office, one of those cozy 80s throwbacks with lots of wood and shelves and books.

"I'm out of ideas," I tell the doctor. "Nothing works. It ruined our entire summer, too. We couldn't go anywhere with him like that."

"Of course. I see." He sits in the corner facing me, a file in his lap, his legs crossed. Beyond the span of windows behind him, the trees sway with a warm gentle September wind.

He lowers his head, nodding slowly, a sign he's thinking. "Actually. There's a new medication I'd like to try. It's new. Only a year old or so. It's been found to be quite effective with this type of irrational fear, or phobia." He tips his head to the side. "Also, it's approved for use with bipolar disorder. So it may help Konner's moods as well."

I feel that sinking sensation again. Of adding another med on top of what Konner is taking these days. At the same time, I know: the phobia's grown into something I can no longer help him with.

"I'll give you some samples," the doctor says, "and send a prescription to your pharmacy."

"You think it'll work?"

He taps the file on his lap with a pen. "Some people do respond well, of course. And others do not. It's the nature of medications, of course. We'll just have to see."

*

A few weeks later, the four of us pile out of the SUV into the parking lot. We head straight for the strip mall ahead and our favorite local Mexican restaurant. Derrick and the boys laugh and joke about lines in a movie they've all watched. I saunter along with the slightest smile, just watching them. Konner looks especially relaxed to me.

I stop, abruptly.

Derrick looks around. "Anything wrong?"

I glance at Konner, who's swinging his arms and laughing, happy. Without looking around.

"Konner," I say.

He stops and looks at me quizzically. "Yeah?"

"Aren't you worried?"

"About what?"

"Bees."

He thrusts his lower jaw out and shrugs. "They haven't really been bothering me much."

When I can't seem to find any words, he waves. "Come on. I'm starving."

Derrick holds out his hand. "You heard the kid,

birthday girl. What do you say we celebrate?"

Chapter 12

Arms Wide Open

I pause at Konner's bedroom door, nervously rubbing one of my thumbs. He's a junior now, a sweet 16, and devotes a lot of his time to music, to playing the keyboard and composing elaborate piano scores. Oh, right,  and he loves to play chess. And solving various Rubik's cubes. That's where I'm

Konner and me, Christmas tree hunting, 2017

going to stop and say *but*.

But he's spending entirely too much time in his room.

The 'c' word, college, looms over the house like a dangling spider. Now that I'm feeling as strong as I am, I wonder how he'll handle college in a year if he can't find a reason to leave his room.

I lift my hand to knock, then pause, afraid of something I haven't seen or heard in years. A screaming fit. I literally can't remember the last time he had one. But I know this little issue I'm about to broach with him is a stressful one. It guarantees *change*. Something Konner never responds to well. And a fit isn't out of the realm of possibility yet.

I knock, give it a second or two, then open the door. And I'm hit by the stale warm air combined with the body odor. My eyes water.

"Woof," I say, and I take a sweeping look at the room. He sits at his desk, oblivious, his earcans on. Around him, popcorn litters the plastic mat under his rolling chair. And a towel and clothes lie strewn about on the dirty rug. Never my favorite things to see. But he's come so far and I'm battled out, so lately I just overlook the mess.

And try to encourage deodorant.

"Hey," I say.

"Oh!" He peels his headcans off and leaves them around his neck. "Sorry. I didn't hear you." His monitor glows with the bright partially finished score he's been working on. Squiggly notes sweep up and down on the white screen behind it. At least it's not a video game, I think to myself. But still. He needs to socialize.

I rub my hand under my nose to combat the smell. "Can we talk a minute?" And maybe open a window? I think.

"Okaaay," he says. He lifts the cans over his head and sets them aside. "That sounds a little too serious." But still. No fit. Despite the interruption this is. No pinched and angry expression. Nothing. It's just my son, my sweet bright son, looking back at me. "Can I play you my new composition first?"

"Sure, let's hear it." I sit on a little corner of his bed, propped on the section of comforter that hasn't slid off it yet.

He reaches for the humming tower beside him, and pulls the headphone jack out. It clicks.

A moment later, a sad and beautiful song spills out of his computer speakers. It's a score with just a hint of Moonlight Sonata to it, by Beethoven, which Konner is practicing daily now, a song he'll play in his school's annual talent show. After a couple of minutes, the song slides into a deep and powerful stretch, then ends with three more deep strong notes.

I'm speechless. It's emotionally beautiful.

The quiet fills my ears and I blink. "Wow," I say. "Gorgeous, Konner. Really well done."

His face lights up as he smiles. "Thanks. So what did you want?"

I rub my thumb, thinking about the words I've practiced. "You're doing so well. I'm proud of you."

"But."

I let out a little laugh, restrained. "Not but. *And. And* I've told you, you need to have an activity. Something you do outside the house. So you're not stuck here in your room all day."

He smashes a hand over his face. "Here we go." But he doesn't shake his fist at me. Or pull back his elbow as if he'll hit me.

"You don't have to ride anymore, okay?" Though it makes me sad at the way he's refused to ride anymore ever since his bee phobia hit. Regardless, I'm not in the business of forcing Konner to do something. Or anything. "I want you to pick something you love."

He opens an eye above his hand. "Like what?"

"Can I read you a list? You get to pick?"

He sighs and lowers his hand. "Fine."

"Swimming?"

"No."

"Golfing?"

"No."

"Cubing?" As in solving the Rubik's cube, competitively.

"No."

"Chess?"

"No. I play that at school."

I take a deep breath. Last one, I think. Or I'm going back to the drawing board. "Theatre acting?"

"Mom." He rolls his eyes. "You know I've always wanted to act."

I let out a sigh. "I do remember." But I also know how his tastes have changed. "So, yes?"

"Yep."

"You mean it?" I say. I've actually won?

He swivels around to his desk again. "As long as I like the play they're doing."

I fold my arms, squeezing myself, and I feel something expand inside. "What if I say that that a cast of teens is doing a dark comedy?"

He twirls around, his eyes big.

I slap the top of my thighs. "Great. I'll sign you up." At his door, I stop and look around. "But, Konner—?"

"Yeah?"

"No quitting, okay? Once you're signed up, you stay to the end."

"Why would I quit?"

Because things get hard. That's why you'd quit. But I don't say it. I'm afraid I'm going to jinx myself.

*

I dial the acting studio.

After a little back and forth, the woman, the owner, apologizes. "We've just closed the cast for that play. I really am sorry."

I hang up and slump at our kitchen table. Please, I whisper. Just one open spot.

Five minutes later, as if my whisper had been carried fifteen miles on a westerly wind, the phone rings. It's the owner of the studio again.

"Kristal?" The woman I spoke to before. "I'm so sorry to bother you, but a young man just called and said he won't be able to act in the play. He's starting college and it's just too much. Would Konner like to take on his roles?"

"Would he?" I say. "I know he'll be thrilled." But I also can't help but warn the woman. I lower my voice, like the words I'm about to say are dirty. "Konner has high-functioning autism. Will that be okay?"

"Oh, sure," she says.

And my whole body goes loose at that.

"I don't know why," the woman continues, "but special needs kids tend to flock to the theatre. We have a couple of others on the spectrum, in fact."

How about that? I stare at a picture of our family that's stuck to our white board, stunned. The play, it seems, is a perfect fit. Hand-picked for Konner. It really is. I just pray he'll really be able to do it.

*

The rest is easy. Smooth, uneventful. Isn't that what I'm supposed to say?

Well, kind of. At first. I drive to rehearsals and sit there, alone, while the kids practice just feet from me. Konner prefers to keep me close and I don't feel comfortable leaving him yet. War wounds, you could say.

But I feel like an amputated limb everyone keeps glancing at, wondering why I'm still sitting there.

For Konner, rehearsals are fun and weekly, just a couple of hours for now, and there isn't a need for Konner to talk to the other kids, so everything's fine. Well, mostly, except for a couple of times when he cries and begs me to let him quit since he has more lines than he realized.

I guess you know what I said to that. "No quitting, bud." I also said we could practice his lines whenever he wants.

Three months later, rehearsals stretch to a full day to gear up for the looming performances (*four* performances, to be exact). I watch Konner's anxiety flare, with a lot more crying and stomping around than I've seen in months, and I'm not really sure how to help him with it.

It's Saturday. All-day rehearsal day. And Derrick and I sit at a friend's 50th birthday party, side by side, enjoying a rare glass of mid-day wine, when Derrick takes out his buzzing phone. Brennig's staying at a friend's all day and Derrick dropped Konner off, alone, at the acting studio early this morning. But both of us know who it will be.

It's the first time we've left him alone there, let alone *anywhere*, and I feel myself cringe when Derrick shows me who's calling him.

It's Konner's cell.

Derrick presses the phone to his ear. "Okay. I know." He listens some more. "It'll take me some time to get there, bud. Can you sit in that little back room and wait?"

Oh well, I think. So much for parties.

Forty-five minutes later, we park and cross a small courtyard that leads to the back of the one-story building.

311

We step into the small back room. There sits Konner, in a small mirrored room, on a wooden bench, eating lunch by himself.

"Can we go?" he says.

I look at Derrick.

"Is the director here?" he says to Konner. "Is it okay with him if you go?"

Konner says, "Yes."

I peer around. Nobody's back here, but I hear a lot of voices out front. It doesn't sound like anyone is leaving yet.

"Maybe," says Derrick, "we should check with him first."

I wait while Derrick and Konner go looking for Jim, the director. Apparently, they bump into him on the way, because all three of them come walking back in.

"Hey, Jim," says Derrick. "Konner was wondering if he could leave."

Jim looks at Konner, evaluating him. He's young and heavy with thinning hair. "Well," he says, "it would be good if you stayed, but I understand if you have to leave." He scratches his head. "We're doing one of your scenes today, though."

He shakes Derrick's hand, then he heads to the front.

Derrick turns back to Konner again. "You know," he says. "You only have a couple of hours left and it's going to go fast."

Konner sighs. "I guess."

"We'll stay close," I say. "We'll wait in the car."

Two hours later, we're standing outside the plate glass windows near the front of the studio. Konner pushes out the door and exits, sweaty and flushed. And grinning, too.

"Glad you stayed?" Derrick says.

Konner is bouncing up and down and talking about the scenes they did. Then he mentions the name of the lead actor, a kid named Luke. "Luke said, 'This is your first play, right?' And I told him, 'Yes.' And he said 'Yeah, well you're pretty good.'"

And Konner's whole attitude changes from there.

*

It's one month later, and the end of Konner's junior year, and Konner decides to squeeze all his victories into a single week. First, he grabs 2nd place in his school chess championship (for the 3rd year in a row, I might add). Second, he sits on a long black bench at his school's annual talent show and plays the deep but gentle tones of

Beethoven's Moonlight Sonata with an emotion that makes

my eyes burn with tears. And, third, he practices nightly with the troupe he's joined, at a small local theatre, where he's joking around and making friends.

Konner, 16, layered in the costumes he wore for the musical, Heathers, 2019

Just two days after his talent show, I stand at the double doors of the tall brick theatre, ten tickets in hand.

I watch two cars pull into the gravel side lot below and I wave to them. I can barely hold my excitement in. In fact, the tickets and the hands I'm using to hold them are trembling.

Derrick's parents and his brother's family, and even my nephew's bashful girlfriend, pile out of the vehicles. They climb the stairs and I hug each one, amazed at what a crowd we have for Konner. "He's so excited you guys could come. Come on, this way." I lead them inside, where I hold the tickets under the scanner, one by one, shaking so hard that the woman has to scan some again.

The theatre's small and soaring, too, and the seats are old-fashioned iron frames with purple cushions. We take up an entire row. A whole row of fans who'll be cheering for Konner, including a mama who hopes, who prays, things don't go wrong that lead to some sort of

*The whole row of seats our family took up
at Konner's play, 2019*

meltdown. Meltdowns are rare, of course, and gentler now,

but they are known to happen in moments of stress.

He's worked so hard to learn his lines, the songs and

all the dance steps. He's been making friends and telling me

how much they make him laugh. He's even enjoyed the

long and daily rehearsals this week. For a kid who was shy

and uncomfortable the day he joined, only four months ago,

he's become so much more confident, even gregarious, with

the rest of the cast. What a change I see when I look at him!

Two hours later, after he delivers all his lines, and changes a few more times than I can keep up with, and there isn't a single meltdown in sight, I leap from my seat and I scream my applause. (It's okay, so does everyone else.)

The first thing he does when the lights come up is jump from the stage and give me a hug.

"Look what you did," I say. "You stuck with it. You never gave up. I'm so proud of you."

He grins practically ear to ear. "Would you say that makes me responsible?"

"Of course! Yes!"

"Can I learn to drive?"

I choke and laugh at the same time.

"Well?"

Little do I know that two months later, he'll be studying to get his driver's permit. And studying for the SATs as well. On his way to hitting the same major milestones any mainstream kid would hit. Well, how about that?

*

On vacation one night a few weeks later, with the sun setting over the grassy Hilton Head bay around us, I point to a piece of calamari the waiter has brought. I'd elbow Konner but he might not like that. So instead, I wink. "Dare you to try it."

"Uh-uh." He shakes his head. "I specifically said no to seafood on this trip, Mom."

"One small piece." I hold up my thumb and forefinger, just a sliver of space between the two. "But you have to chew it and taste it, too."

He laughs. "You couldn't pay me enough."

Oh no? I wiggle my shoulders. "How about fifty bucks?"

He sticks his neck way back, surprised, eyebrows raised, and stares at me with his chocolatey eyes. To see if I'm joking.

I'm not, though. Remember, I'm a terrible mom. And sometimes I do terrible things. Like bribe my son. Though I think this is likely my first attempt.

"Seriously?" Konner says.

"Seriously." I glance at Derrick who rolls his eyes. But, frankly, I'm dying to see what Konner does with this.

He grabs a fried calamari ring and pops it in, then he chews with a squinty grossed-out expression. He chews. And chews. And swallows the thing.

I press my palms to my cheeks, still warm from the setting sun, and watch him suck an entire glass of root beer down through a paper straw. "Dude," I say, and I lower my hands.

"Proud of you, bud." Derrick says.

Konner shivers. "Blech. That was gross."

I laugh into the palm of my hand. "And you chewed it enough to know it was gross. So I know you actually tasted it."

I glance at Brennig across the table. He sits with perfectly squared poise, his gelled blond hair swept to the side, and shakes his head as he looks at me, this boy who loves trying new things as much as he loves hitting the shops with his Mom. Oops. Did I actually say that?

"Don't worry," I say. "You'll get the same as Konner's getting."

He gives me a look of discomfort, this boy. "No thanks," he says. "I don't need to be bribed."

"I know you don't." So I give him a broad and guilty grin and I finally fess up. "I was going to give you both spending money for the trip anyway." I nod at Konner. "You see that, though?"

Derrick's shaking his head now. At my pure rationalized ridiculousness.

And I know how the naughty cat felt now, with the canary feathers still sticking from its mouth. But it tasted so good, that victory.

Maybe it's not as huge a coup to anyone else as it is to me. And maybe the bribery's bad, bad, bad. But I tell you because I want you to know: The sweet and uproariously funny Konner I'm living with now is not the aggressive unpredictable Konner I lived with for most of his growing up years. He's still a bit rigid about some things. But he's flexible, too.

And once in a while he'll try something new.

*

It's hard not to get choked up over the changes we've seen. In Konner, of course. In the everyday lives we finally lead. And even in myself. I'm stronger and more appreciative.

Not long after we've gotten home from vacation again, I sit on my bed to put on my shoes.

Behind me, I hear a knock on the frame of my open door.

Konner walks in. "Hey."

"What's up?"

"This." He leans over and hugs me hard. "You're the greatest Mom in the world," he says. "I couldn't have wished for a better Mom than you."

I sit there, stunned, at what he's just said. Especially since I'd struggled with feeling like a terrible mom in the midst of his pain. My eyes blur and I realize, after years of fighting to get Konner to feel his best, we've arrived. At his best. At his absolute best.

It's a far cry from that day at the fire station, when I told Konner he had to get out of the car. It's a far cry from the days I wished I could walk away from him, too. Thank God I stuck with it. Thank God I'm his mom.

Chapter 13

A Combat-Ready Arsenal

For twelve long years, my husband and I

struggled day and night to find the right doctor, the right

mix of meds, the right small private challenging school, the

right activities Konner loves, you name it, the things that

would soothe the raging beast and cause it to spit our son

back out.

If we hadn't done that, what do you think we'd see

today, at age 17? Would we see a kid with a gun in his

hand, jogging into a middle school? Or would we be sitting

slumped by his grave, years after he'd swallowed too many

pills or, worse, used one of our kitchen knives?

Sorry, I see you wincing there.

But those were things I worried myself sick about. Until we found the right mix of things that worked for our son.

Thank God, of course, those things didn't happen to

 him or to us.

We weathered the storm and came out alive. With a few singe marks and scars, perhaps. But, seriously, most of the time, we're *good.*

Konner, 16, after playing Beethoven's Moonlight Sonata at his school's talent show, 2019

Did we do the right things to free our son, our treasure, our heart, from the monstrous rage that swallowed him whole? Mostly, yes. I believe we did. And my proof is in the pictures you'll see at the end of this book. In the smiles, the bright unabashed smiles, my son wears when you look at him now.

Have we lived through our time in hell and reached some form of divine perfection? Certainly not. I'm flawed, as flawed as a mother comes. I'm selfish at times. I want my own space. And I lose my temper if it's almost dinner and Konner hasn't emptied the dishwasher yet. (Sorry, just keeping things real here).

Konner is Konner. The person he was always meant to be. Despite the solutions we've found to help, he'll always have autism spectrum disorder. That's just who he is. He'll always be perfectly special that way. But I'll always worry about him, too. Will he be able to handle college? A job? A wife and kids?

And then I remember.

One day, ages and ages ago, he asked if he'd be able to go to college one day. And I said back then, "Baby, you'll do the same things everyone else can do, maybe a little bit later sometimes, but as soon as you're ready." And, now, he's studying for the SATs. And planning to apply to a college that has an incredible autism support program. At the same time everybody else his age is heading to college. Right on time.

Yes, he'll be able to handle college. A job. A family. All those things. How could I even question that? He'll do all the same things everybody else can do. And more. And I'll cry with every success he has.

Does he still have things that trigger him? We all do, right? And he's no different. Mostly, it's things that make him feel overstimulated. Too many sounds or too many people or too many things he needs to do. And sometimes the thing that sets him off is his good ole mom, telling him too many things at once.

But the good news here is he's learned to cope, to soothe himself, to ask for space, and that by itself is a victory.

As I've said before, there's a reason for that, that victory. We found a mishmash of things that worked. Things that stripped the terrible away, revealing the wonderfully affectionate and funny boy underneath, setting him free from the prison of flesh and hormones and bone that had caged him in.

So here's where I list what worked for us. And I purposely use the word 'us' here, knowing that what worked for Konner might not work the exact same way for another child. Each child is as unique in their internal chemistry as they are in their personality. But I do believe, and strongly at that, that each child has a mix of things that will work. It's just a matter of trial and error and of finding it.

For us that trial started with prayer. And not just some words we shot at the sky. At times, I knelt at the foot of Konner's bed in the dark as he slept at night. And I whispered my fiercest battle prayers.

Did they work? Oh yes. There's power in prayer. And so many people were praying along. And our prayers were answered one after another in his junior year, years after I'd stopped expecting answers to some of them. Just look at my son's smile, you'll see it. The freedom and the joy you'll see on his face. If you ask me to show you a miracle, I'll show you my son.

After that, the mix that worked for us best was amazingly clear:

- **The right child psychiatrist**. Not all psychiatrists
  are created equal. I'm afraid the best don't take
  insurance. It was worth it for us to pay that price,
  and it still is. We've seen five psychiatrists over the
  years. Only one had a plan and knew what to do.

- **The right mix of meds**. I can't say this enough.
  Without the right meds, it all falls apart For Konner,
  that is. The meds treat the illness inside his brain.
  The mood disorder. And the fear and anxiety that's
  at its root. Without the right meds, Konner is sick.
  And that sickness is a terribly scary thing. For
  Konner we currently use a mix of mood stabilizers,
  an anti-depressant, a stimulant (for ADHD and his
  impulsivity), a blood pressure medicine which
  relaxes him and an anti-psychotic which helps with
  his moods and phobias. Six medications treat the
  different parts of his brain affected. As well as an

anti-anxiety medication he's allowed to use on demand when needed (though he rarely needs it). It was a long, painstaking methodical process to get him onto the meds he's on. But he's doing so well, we're pulling him off one of his meds, stepping down slowly every two weeks, to see if he can handle life without it. But, still, meds work. For his illness. They work. And we use them because we have to. Because of his illness. That's that.

- **The right small school**. It's made such a difference. We quickly saw that a small flexible environment works best, a school that knows how to deescalate a child who's in distress. A school with smart and compassionate staff and challenging courses. And not one that uses discipline and prison cells as its main solution. For Konner, that school (or high school at least) has a 6-1-1 environment:

No more than six students sit in a class, along with a teacher and full-time aide. I equate looking for a school to finding a home. It'll either feel like a home. Or it won't. Don't settle.

- **Communicating Konner's needs to his school,** which I've talked about. But see the next chapter for a letter you can customize and give to your child's own school.

- **A healthy diet, within reason at least.** And, believe me, if it's a diet, I've already tried it. Gluten free. Lactose-free. Soy-free. The ADHD Feingold diet. The GAPS diet. The Paleo diet. Taking raw probiotics in capsule form, as well as raw homemade probiotic drinks like water kefir and kombucha (great stuff). Cooking everything we eat from scratch, with nothing processed. Do you know what that got us? Healthy. Very healthy, indeed. But I just about keeled over from the sheer exhaustion of cooking. I did. And, as it turned out, none of it helped Konner's moods. (Except for protein. Lots of protein. Protein helped.) So I'll just say this: If you try a diet and it works, great! If it doesn't, just keep the whole eating thing as sane and simple as possible. And I mean that. Sane. Life has enough battles as it is.

- **Consistent consequences**. By this I mean the kind of practical common-sense consequences I learned to come up with whenever Konner misbehaved. Like this: Okay, I warned you. You're acting up. We're not stopping for that treat now. (Then lots of screaming and kicking ensues). You're not going to get out of bed for school? Okay. Give me your phone for the rest of the day. If it seems to make

334

sense, that's what I try.

- **The right outside activities**. For Konner, at first, it was horseback riding. For five great years. It was something he loved that made him smile. For a short time, he did nothing at all. The bugs easily saw to that. Now, he prefers piano and acting. My rule is this: He has to do something. But it also has to be something he loves.

- **Weekly counseling visits**. For years. Just know it's not a quick solution to a problem for kids, especially young kids. It's someone to guide and listen to them. But, a warning, too. I learned the hard way not to share a psychologist with Konner. It created a conflict of interest at times, especially when a counselor disagreed with a doctor's office or with my personal parenting approach. When I talk to a counselor, I want them to listen to *me*, to the struggles I'm going through. And I want Konner's counselor to listen to him. No tug-of-wars.

Okay, so say you're going to try all the things I listed here. Will it work for you?

I believe it will. I honestly do. Every child is different, complex, with their own individual needs. But I have no doubt that a mix of the things that worked for our son will work for other children like him, small angry explosive kids.

If you start with my template and work from there, I believe you'll see significant improvement in your child's own behavior, perhaps more quickly than my own son did.

And, honestly, what do you have to lose?

Chapter 14

A Letter to the School

Having a child who can't communicate when he's upset means that most of the communication falls to me as his advocate. As his mom and primary caretaker, it's my responsibility to educate the staff of Konner's schools and others about his condition, letting them know what types of things help diffuse an emotionally overheated situation.

Here's a copy (amended) of the instructional letter I gave to one of Konner's middle schools, as I've talked about, after an assistant teacher upset him, things escalated, and he finally bit a security guard (he was lucky he didn't get tasered, no?) The list is common sense, in a way, and yet opposite of the way most mainstream schools try to handle violent kids who have emotional issues. They usually choose to penalize or clamp down on inappropriate behavior, when that in fact will escalate things.

Feel free to use a letter like this with your child's school, amended as needed, to reflect special tactics that work with your child.

Konner and his dad in Hilton Head, SC, in 2019

Dear [Administrator/School], Date

I'm writing this letter in follow-up to the incident [my child] had at school on [date]. What you were dealing with that day was [my child's] illness, a [mood disorder related to his autism spectrum disorder/insert your own diagnosis here].

[My child] is responsible for his actions that day. However, we need to have another way of dealing with things when [my child] is upset. Based on the sequence of events that day, I believe the incident did not need to escalate to the point that it did.

When it comes to [my child's] illness, de-escalation is key. If you would, think of [my child] as a pot of very hot water when he's upset; how you respond to him will either cause him to cool down or boil over. With that said, I have included some background information on [my child]

339

here, and some practical steps you can follow to help deescalate a situation if it arises.

Background on [my child]:

[My child] has a [mood disorder/insert your own diagnosis here], meaning:

- He cannot regulate his moods on his own
- He feels his moods many times more strongly than a typical child
- He has tremendous difficulty controlling himself when he is upset
- He can't communicate when he's upset

Aggravating factors:

- Puberty and hormone changes will aggravate his illness as he grows

- Any major change tends to affect him; the more prepared he is, the better

- Looming holidays and school-year transitions affect him, and his excitement may come through as anger/irritability

- The change in seasons (lack of sunlight, warmth) affect him

- [My child] is easily embarrassed

- He is easily confused when there is too much stimulation

- He cannot communicate what he feels, thinks or needs when he is feeling upset

- When he's feeling well (mood-wise), he tends to perform well, behave well and follow the rules

- When he's not feeling well (mood-wise), it directly affects his performance, behavior and ability to comply

How to help [my child] when he is agitated/upset:

- *Hand signal:* Create <u>a private hand signal</u> that [my child] can use with staff to let them know he's getting upset and needs some space.

- *Time and space: Give him <u>time</u> and <u>space</u> to calm down (think silence and privacy but not confinement).*
  - ○ Don't ask him too many questions at once (either repetitively or in quick succession).
  - ○ Don't expect him to be able to talk to you right away.
  - ○ Don't overwhelm him with too many people hovering over him in the same room.

- *Safe people: Designate <u>a list of 'safe people'</u> who can go to him (or who he can go to) to help calm* *him down when he's upset (much like a child who's*

having an asthma attack); don't expect him to be

able to come to you (when he's upset he may not be

able to).

    o   Here is a list of adults in school I know he

        trusts: [list names here]

- ***Safe place:*** *Designate a 'safe place' where [my*

  *child] can be relatively **alone**, where he doesn't feel*

  like people are looking at him, but can still be

  monitored for safety reasons. For example, a

  conference room.

- ***Walk around:*** *Take him for a walk so he can move*

  around, get air and vent, if needed (when he's not

  feeling as agitated).

- ***Listen:*** When he is calm and able to talk, give him

  the chance to be heard first and to tell his side of the

  story.

- ***Call me:*** If you need to call, please <u>make sure [my child] is not in the room at the time</u>:
  - He does not like to hear people talking about him when he has made a mistake (he's easily embarrassed, which makes him upset).
  - It would be best if an adult called me privately to tell me what happened, before allowing [my child] to speak to me separately one-on-one (not on speaker).

I appreciate all the time and energy you've spent working to support [my child.] I hope you find the tactics listed in this letter helpful. Please don't hesitate to call with questions.

All the best,

[Your name], [relationship to child], [best phone number to

reach you at]

Chapter 15

Talk About 'Mental'

Imagine this. You take your two-year-old child to a doctor, to treat what you think is a broken wrist. You can see it's hot and swollen and red. Three times its size. And the child cries out each time the wrist is touched or bent. But x-rays don't exist. Not yet.

Konner, 2, at a lake in Massachusetts, 2004

The doctor frowns, nodding. "I see. What you have is a difficult child here. Nothing wrong with his wrist." He scribbles a note, rips off a sheet and hands it to you. "Just give him a practical consequence whenever he tantrums about that wrist. Timeout. No treat. Just pick a punishment off that sheet." He smiles and waves to your weeping child and leaves the room.

Awful. I know.

You know I'm going somewhere with this. I know you do. Okay, let's take that same two-year-old child and force them to go to school. Preschool. Or daycare, perhaps. Even just for a couple of hours. Then sports. Or a party. A trip to the store. Or whatever activities you're going to drag him through that day. How do you think your child is going to respond to that? With screaming? Kicking? Meltdowns? Check.

Stay with me here.

347

What if, instead of a broken wrist, that child has a real and crippling disease that's based in the brain? A disease that can't be x-rayed yet. Or put in a cast while it mends itself. A ghastly disease that might respond to some heavy meds, except each med is really a dart you throw at a board, to see what sticks. Sounds a bit like a guessing game, right? And yet, perhaps, it's a slow, methodical guessing game, led by a doctor who knows the disease and its symptoms, and how to get some results.

That was my son. You know that, of course. But the analogy applies to a lot more kids who haven't been accurately diagnosed, understood or helped. Kids who are labeled as 'bad' or 'psycho,' who have a crippling and unstable illness. A physical illness, based in the brain.

So what do we do?

I'm by no means an expert on all the mass shootings we've seen in our nation, or on guns and violence, and I'm certainly no expert on healthcare reform or how to solve the crisis of (gag, we're still calling it) 'mental illness.' But I see something's wrong in our nation today. And I'm sick of the stigma attached to these debilitating brain diseases people call 'mental.' Still, I'm no expert in any of that.

My expertise comes from living through twelve long years of hell with a boy who was angry and violent all day. A boy who scared me out of my mind.

I'm an expert because I lived through it all, and I learned and changed. So did my son. We lived to see what worked for his crippling mood disorder, a condition closely entangled with his autism spectrum disorder. I'm an expert in finding what worked. I am. And, unfortunately, I'm also an expert in the loneliness that stemmed from that, from the stigma of having a violent child. The horrified eyes. Judgmental looks. The looks that blamed me for being an awful parent to him. I'm an expert because I lived it, okay? And I know there are others living it, too.

Lots of others who need our help.

So what do we do in our nation today, to stop the violent trends we're seeing? The ones related to (cough, gag) 'mental illness.' I'll give you my thoughts. Just a few, I promise. But, remember, they're just the thoughts of a mom who knew where her son was headed if he hadn't been drastically healed.

Obliterate the Whole 'Mental' Thing

First, and foremost, we need to take a sledgehammer to the whole 'mental illness' label. These are brain diseases. Not sick and twisted idiocies. They're diseases that attack an organ, the brain, in much the way a cancer does. So what do we do? We educate the heck out of people, in schools, ads, books, movies, blogs, magazines, you name it, keep going. If you've had a significant brain disease, like depression, anxiety, bipolar, schizophrenia, PTSD, and tons, tons more, please, I beg you, tell your story. That's what we need. We need to bring these diseases out of the Dark Ages. By telling our stories. By telling the *truth*.

Educate our Educators

I live in a state that, supposedly, is doing a much better job in the area of special education than a lot of states. And in some areas, I'd agree with that. There are a lot of great schools and programs that fit the needs of so many students. However. And, yes, that's a big however. Children like Konner are quickly misunderstood and judged. First graders in the news in handcuffs, hello? And misjudging a child can quickly escalate a situation to something much worse when the staff and teachers in our schools don't know how to properly diffuse an emotional child.

Oh, and who should I lay into about the use of prison-like quiet rooms in special-ed schools. All I have to say is: The people who run those facilities ought to be ashamed of themselves. Start with preventive measures, people, and tactics at diffusing heated situations, and see how much more you can do without cells.

Invest in Research

We need to invest in brain disease research the way we've invested in cancer. Hello? I can see the momentum starting to build, but we need to be doing so much more. More treatments like TMS, for starters. Who do I need to call to make that happen? Help!

Educate the Medical Community

Let's train up an army of doctors and nurses who know these diseases inside and out. And pay them well. Believe you me, I've been to in-network psychiatrists before. There's a reason the better psychiatrists aren't taking insurance today. They don't get paid for the time they put into seeing the really complex cases.

Get Smart About Healthcare Reform

I'm sorry, but we need to make healthcare truly affordable. For everyone. Healthcare that happens to cover the diseases I'm talking about. And let's stop breaking out 'mental health benefits' separately, please? For heaven's sake. The brain's an organ in the body, no? A physical piece of our physical health. So why doesn't it count as a body part when it happens to have a brain disease?

Okay, that's enough. I'll end my rant before I get myself really in trouble. I hope you agree that something needs to be done. I do. But I'll leave you with lots to think and, hopefully, talk about. The more people are willing to talk about the stigma of (sigh) 'mental illness' and the brain diseases they've suffered from, the closer we'll get to helping the people who aren't getting help right now.

Now is the time to tackle this issue. We have to. Now. Before this crisis turns into another national tragedy.

Chapter 16

Look at Us Now

Our family visiting Hilton Head Island, SC, 2019

I'm so thrilled you hung in there to watch all our

monstrous battles and a small handful of miraculous saves,

to see how we came out victorious. While I don't have the

space to tell you about every horror we faced, I think

you've gotten a pretty good picture of what went on and

how much we've had to overcome to free our son from his

mood disorder.

And he's free. He's free! Thank God, he's free.

I hope you feel encouraged, too. Because good things always come from the bad. This book, for instance, which I'm hoping will help others understand how these monster children are suffering, and everyone else who's touched by their lives, whether good or bad.

Is this the battle you're going through with your own child? There's help. There's hope. Please don't give up! Keep trying, keep fighting, you'll find what works.

Is this battle something that's new to you? I hope you've learned not only what monster children are like, but you see that even the worst situations in life can be faced and overcome when we work together, along with our schools and communities, with the patience and compassion everyone deserves.

So how has our family ended up after all these years? The truth is, we're not perfect. We're not. We're better, I think. Better than before. We have weaknesses, flaws, and we even know how to deal with a few. We face them head on. It's the only way. And we have more good days than bad, for sure.

To be honest, I still get annoyed at Konner's behavior at times. (Sorry, it's true.) I still get annoyed that he won't shower and wash his hair, that he, oops, decided to stop brushing his teeth (for a year), oops!; that he, oops, insists on eating too many carbs and the same five things in a day, how he, oops, would rather sit in a room with the windows closed and sweat through his shirts, in front of his glowing monitor, than go out swimming with the rest of us.

Do I fight each and every battle? No. I fight the ones I think are worth it, then I leave the rest for another day. But here's the kicker. Our house is peaceful most of

Our family visiting Savannah, GA, 2019

the time. No screaming. No hitting. No fear of what Konner is going to do.

We love to eat out as a family, at our favorite local Mexican place or even outside (despite the threat of mosquitoes, too!) on our recent vacation to Hilton Head.

Oh, and we took one of those cool carriage tours of historic

Savannah, Georgia, and really enjoyed ourselves.

Right now, I'm listening to Konner and Derrick

watch an explosive action movie, while eating some

homemade popcorn Konner cooked on the stove.

So what is Konner up to? He's studying hard for the

SATs, online no less, and he's reading up on the rules of

the road to get ready to test for his driver's permit. He even

(shhh) drove a car one day, with Derrick showing him what

to do. He almost hit the garage, yeah, oops! But he hit the

brakes at the last minute and triumphed. Yay!

Does he still take meds? A handful a day. But

we've learned his quality of life (and ours) is too important

to put off until sometime tomorrow, and we trust the future

will take care of itself, without trying to worry about it. For

now, he's well, so wonderfully well, that his psychiatrist is

slowly, cautiously stepping him down from one of his very

first meds for the very first time. It's a scary exciting step for me (and Konner, of course). Because, if he's able to come off one, perhaps he can come off another one, too.

So we work our hardest to help him feel his absolute best. We listen to the wisdom of the specialists God's put in our path, and we pray the results will be favorable. Yes. That's what we do.

What about me? Is my writing going any better these days? Well, you tell me. You're reading this book, so you probably know, but I'll tell you a secret. I happen to be working on a novel, too, a dark sci-fi (horror!) book for younger tweens. Aside from that, I'm waiting to hear from a publisher and a national contest to see if some of my shorter works are as good as I hope. Fingers crossed.

Will you cross your fingers along with me, or say a quick prayer? I'll be praying for you and your family, for sure, especially if you're battling a monster of your own.

You can do it. Don't stop. Every child is different. But you'll find what works. Just as long as you don't let your fears of what other people think stop you from trying out things you think might help.

My handsome guys, 2019

And, you know what else? Send me an email to let me know how you're doing. Please. At kristal@kristaljohnson.com. I'll do my best to respond in a reasonable amount of time. Just give me some time. I've been through a ton, and I don't move as fast as I used to. (And, thankfully, I no longer have to. Yay!)

Konner with his dad at an amusement park in 2019

With my heart, my son, 2019